OFFICIALLY WITHDRAWN
West Allegheny
High School Library

CAREERS
IN
THE
US ARMED
FORCES

CAREERS IN THE
US NAVY

Taylor Baldwin Kiland

OFFICIALLY WITHDRAWN
West Allegheny
High School Library

 Enslow Publishing
101 W. 23rd Street
Suite 240
New York, NY 10011
USA
enslow.com

This book is dedicated to all those brave men and women serving around the world in the US Navy today.

Published in 2016 by Enslow Publishing, LLC
101 W. 23rd Street, Suite 240, New York, NY 10011

Copyright © 2016 by Taylor Baldwin Kiland

All rights reserved.

No part of this book may be reproduced by any means
without the written permission of the publisher.

Library of Congress Cataloging-in-Publication Data

Kiland, Taylor Baldwin, 1966-
  Careers in the US Navy / Taylor Baldwin Kiland.
    pages cm. — (Careers in the US Armed Forces)
  Includes bibliographical references and index.
  Summary: "Describes career opportunities in the US Navy"—Provided by publisher.
  Audience: Grades 7-8.
  ISBN 978-0-7660-6949-7
  1. United States. Navy—Vocational guidance—Juvenile literature. 2. United States. Navy—Juvenile literature.
  I. Title.
  VB259.K55 2015
  359.0023'73—dc23

                                    2015015140

Printed in the United States of America

To Our Readers: We have done our best to make sure all Web site addresses in this book were active and appropriate when we went to press. However, the author and the publisher have no control over and assume no liability for the material available on those Web sites or on any Web sites they may link to. Any comments or suggestions can be sent by e-mail to customerservice@enslow.com.

Portions of this book originally appeared in the book *The U.S. Navy and Military Careers*.

Photo Credits: © AP Images, p. 50; bikeriderlondon/Shutterstock.com, p. 1 (Navy officers); Bonnie Real/NASA Images/archive.org, p. 72; Christine Yarusi, p. 1 (series logo); Daniel Baker, US Navy/Wikimedia Commons/2010 Haiti earthquake relief efforts by the US Army.jpg/public domain, p. 64; DoD photo by Petty Officer 3rd Class Sammy Dallal, US Navy, p. 60; DoD photo by Staff Sgt. Jim Goodwin, US Marine Corps, p. 101; Everett Historical/Shutterstock.com, p. 17; GrummelJS/Wikimedia Commons/Michael Mullen Donald Winter Terry Scott.jpg/public domain, p. 66; Jerry Grayson/Helifilms Australia PTY Ltd/Getty Images, p. 62; Library of Congress, Prints and Photographs Division, p. 21; Library of Congress, Prints & Photographs Division, FSA/OWI Collection, [LC-USW33-018433-C], p. 42 ; MPI/Stringer/Archive Photos/Getty Images, p. 29; Naval History & Heritage/US Naval Institute, p. 74; Popperfoto/Getty Images, p. 33; Schlendrian/US Navy photo courtesy of US Naval Historical Center/Wikimedia Commons/USS George Washington (SSBN-598).jpg/public domain, p. 52; Sheldon Levis/Photolibrary/Getty Images, p. 23; SimonATL/Naval Historic Center/Wikimedia Commons/Tr great white fleet tr addresses USS Connecticut Feb 1909.jpg/public domain, p. 35; Steve Cukrov/Shutterstock.com (chapter openers); The Print Collector/Print Collector/Hulton Archive/Getty Images, p. 34; Time Life Pictures/US Navy/The LIFE Picture Collection/Getty Images, p. 44; US Naval Historical Center Photograph # NH 85735. Courtesy of Alfred Cellier, 1977, p. 31; US Navy photo, pp. 11, 40, 77; US Navy photo by Chief Mass Communication Specialist Steve Johnson, p. 82; US Navy photo by Chief Photographer's Mate Chris Desmond, p. 85; US Navy photo by Chief Photographer's Mate Spike Call , p. 109; US Navy photo by Chief Photographer's Mate Todd P. Cichonowicz, p. 111; US Navy photo courtesy of NASA, p. 115; US Navy photo by Journalist Seaman Erica Mater, p. 100; US Navy photo by Mass Communication Specialist 1st Class Chad Runge, p. 86; US Navy photo by Mass Communication Specialist 1st Class Michael D. Kennedy, p. 70; US Navy photo by Mass Communication Specialist 1st Class N. Ross Taylor, p. 95; US Navy photo by Mass Communication Specialist Seaman Adam K. Thomas, pp. 12; US Navy photo by Mass Communication Specialist Seaman Christopher D. Gaines, p. 89; US Navy Photo by Mass Communication Specialist 3rd Class Ignacio D. Perez, p. 90; US Navy Photo by Mass Communication Specialist 3rd Class Jackie Hart, p. 84; US Navy photo by Mass Communication Specialist 3rd Class Jake Berenguer, p. 76; US Navy photo by Mass Communication Specialist 3rd Class Johans Chavarro, p. 113; US Navy photo by Mass Communication Specialist 3rd Class Maddelin Angebrand, p. 108; US Navy photo by Mass Communication Specialist 3rd Class Marcus L. Stanley, p. 94; US Navy photo by Mass Communication Specialist 3rd Class Tyler Thompson, p. 106; US Navy photo by Petty Officer 2nd Class Matt Daniels, p. 7; US Navy photo by Photographer's Mate Airman Javier Capella, p. 92; US Navy photo by Photographer's Mate Airman Joshua Olson, p. 68; US Navy photo by Photographers Mate 1st Class Andy McKaskle, p. 104; US Navy photo by Photographer's Mate 3rd Class Rebecca J. Moat, p. 61; US Navy photo by Photographer's Mate 3rd Class Summer M. Anderson, pp. 58, 67; US Navy photo by Sue Krawczyk, p. 83; Valerie Macon/Getty Images Entertainment/Getty Images, p. 10.

Cover Credits: bikeriderlondon/Shutterstock.com (top); US Navy photo by Mass Communication Specialist 3rd Class Kevin V. Cunningham (bottom); Christine Yarusi (series logo).

CONTENTS

Acknowledgments

This book could not have been written without the expert review and advice, the keen eyes and imaginations of several young readers who served as the official "focus group" for this book: Katie Bennett, Mac Hayes, Shepp McCain, Ian Richards, and Marie Smeallie.

Special thanks to Lieutenant Commander Jeff Bender, USN; Lieutenant Bill Davis, USN; Hospital Corpsman Second Class Jason Deaver, USN; Lieutenant Matt Galan, USN; Lieutenant John Gay, USN; the Commanding Officer and crew of the USS *George Washington*; Mark Hacala; Humza Kamzi; Ed Kearle; Lieutenant Commander Julie Kellogg, MC, USN; Lieutenant Commander Dave Larsen, USN; Admiral Henry C. Mauz, USN (Ret.); Commander John B. Mustin, USNR, Commanding Officer of IBU-22; the crew of IBU-22; the Navy Office of Information; Master at Arms First Class Greg Pratt, US; Lieutenant (j.g.) Leslie Smith, USN; the Navy Recruiting Command; and Captain Kevin Wensing, USN.

THE LONE SURVIVOR

Any man who may be asked in this century what he did to make his life worthwhile ... can respond with a good deal of pride and satisfaction, "I served in the United States Navy."

—President John F. Kennedy, former naval officer[1]

Dangling from a Chinook transport helicopter twenty feet above ground in a moonless night, Navy Petty Officer Marcus Luttrell and three other Navy sailors—Petty Officer Matthew Axelson, Petty Officer Danny Dietz, and Lieutenant Michael Murphy, "fast roped" onto the side of a remote mountain in northeastern Afghanistan, near the border of Pakistan. It was June 28, 2005, and the four men were on a mission, called

Operation Red Wings, to find and kill Ahmad Shah, a Taliban leader in the region. The elite four-man special operations team started their hike in the dark and cold rain to find Shah. They struggled to maintain their footing in the mud and to see where they were going in the downpour. They also needed to stay hidden.

After the sun came up, they burrowed their mud-caked bodies behind some rocks and tree stumps, lying prone in an area where they could see into the valley below to Ahmad Shah's suspected location. "It was deathly quiet up there, just as silent as the night," Petty Officer Luttrell remembers. "And just as suddenly, there was a guy, wearing a turban and carrying a[n]...ax. He jumped off the log, right over top of me. I damn near fainted with shock." Petty Officer Luttrell turned his rifle on the man and ordered him to sit down. "And then something ridiculous happened. About a hundred goats, all with little bells around their necks, came trotting up the mountain, swarming all around the spot where we were now standing. Then up the hill came two more guys. All of us were now surrounded by goats."[2] And the three goat herders —one of whom was a young boy, who could reveal their location to the local Taliban.

Now that their mission was compromised, the men faced a dilemma. If they killed the unarmed men, it would be immoral and would violate the US military's rules of engagement. If they let them go, the goat herders could inform the local Taliban forces. They let them go and quickly tried to find a way to defend their position and call back to the base for reinforcements. But, within one hour, dozens of Shah's forces appeared over the mountain ridgeline and launched an avalanche of grenade and mortar attacks. And the terrain was

A team of US Navy SEALs fly suspended from a helicopter during a patrol insertion and extraction exercise.

just as hostile: as the SEALs scrambled to evade the incoming rounds, they fell and jumped hundreds of feet down the mountain, breaking and fracturing bones.

Petty Officer Dietz was shot multiple times. As Petty Officer Luttrell hoisted him onto his shoulders to carry him down the mountain, a bullet hit Petty Officer Dietz in the back of the head and killed him instantly. Lieutenant Murphy was also badly wounded and knew the four men needed help. But his communications gear was not working well. The only place he could get a workable radio connection was to walk or crawl out to an exposed clearing, where he quickly called for back-up—but not before he was felled by a bullet that hit him in the back. He managed to continue talking on the phone to let his unit commanders identify the men's location, but he could not survive his wounds.

Petty Officers Luttrell and Axelson found a spot to hide and Luttrell, a trained medic, tried to help Petty Officer Axelson, who had a severe head wound. But a rocket-propelled grenade blew them both into the air. Luttrell survived the blast, but he never saw Axelson again.

Lieutenant Murphy's call for help alerted his fellow SEALs that the four men were in dire need of help. They rushed two Chinook helicopters carrying special operations forces to the scene. Tragically, a rocket-propelled grenade shot one of them out of the air, killing eight SEALs and eight Army Night Stalkers.

As the sun set, nineteen Americans were dead and no one knew Petty Officer Luttrell was the lone survivor. Despite a broken back, bullet wounds, and rocks and shrapnel protruding from his legs, he crawled seven miles through the mountains, evading capture by killing anyone who came near him.

Starving, thirsty, and light-headed from losing blood, he stumbled upon a waterfall and attempted to quench his thirst—oblivious to his surroundings for a few moments. And he was caught—surrounded by a group of local men. This time, however, he was lucky. They were friendly. One of the men, Mohammad Gulab, convinced Luttrell that they were not Taliban and they wanted to help him. Gulab and several men carried Luttrell back to their village and gave him food, water, and shelter. They also defended the village from Taliban who surrounded the village, demanding that the villagers turn over their guest, the American. Gulab and his fellow villages refused and hid Luttrell for four days, protecting him until a message written by Luttrell could be transported to a Marine outpost.

With news that Luttrell was alive, the military initiated a massive search-and-rescue operation to rescue Luttrell with aircraft and ground forces. Assisted by his new friend Gulab, Luttrell limped to a waiting helicopter that evacuated him to an American base to recover.

Petty Officer Luttrell was the lone survivor of Operation Red Wings. For his actions, he received the Navy Cross, the Navy's second highest award. Petty Officers Axelson and Dietz received the same award posthumously. Lieutenant Murphy posthumously received the nation's highest military honor, the Medal of Honor.

All four of these men were SEALs, members of the Navy SEa, Air, Land teams, the Navy's principal special operations force. Their mission is to conduct small-unit maritime operations and they operate where large ships and submarines cannot due to water depth. They train to work in extreme climates—scorching desert, freezing Arctic, and humid jungle. In the Global War on Terrorism, Navy SEALs have played a critical role in pursuit of elusive, dangerous, and high-priority terrorist targets in the remote mountains of Afghanistan, as well as the urban jungles of Iraq and in hot spots all over the world.

Why Do We Have a Navy?

So, why does the United States have a Navy? Despite its size, the United States has the largest concentration of residents within one hundred miles of its coastline. Although the US Navy was originally founded to defend against the British, the United States has increasingly used naval forces to ensure the safe passage of commercial ships around the world. In

Marcus Luttrell (left) attends the Hollywood premiere for *Lone Survivor*, the movie based on his experience fighting the Taliban in Operation Redwing, in 2013.

This photo shows Marcus Luttrell with his fellow Navy SEALs, all of whom perished in Operation Red Wing. From left to right, Sonar Technician (Surface) 2nd Class Matthew G. Axelson, of Cupertino, Calif; Senior Chief Information Systems Technician Daniel R. Healy, of Exeter, N.H.; Quartermaster 2nd Class James Suh, of Deerfield Beach, Fla.; Hospital Corpsman 2nd Class Marcus Luttrell; Machinists Mate 2nd Class Eric S. Patton, of Boulder City, Nev.; and Lt. Michael P. Murphy, of Patchogue, N.Y.

The US Navy has a long and proud heritage. Here, sailors man the rails aboard the aircraft carrier USS *George Washington*.

other words, the US Navy patrols the world to make sure that the United States can have the products and services that fuel its economy and lifestyle. The US Navy also operates throughout the world where the United States' vital interests may be threatened. The US Navy helps build alliances with friendly countries and deters potential aggressors from taking hostile action against the United States.

While the US Navy has been on duty to defend the nation's interests and to help its allies in world conflicts for more than two centuries, the war on terrorism began in earnest after the country was attacked on September 11, 2001. The war has tested the armed forces, including the Navy, like no other challenge. The Navy's additional missions now include intercepting and stopping terrorist acts before they occur and supporting American and allied ground forces engaged in combat operations against terrorists and other enemies.

A select few citizens have been devoting their lives to this cause, the US Navy. Petty Officer Luttrell is a sterling example. American citizens, like Luttrell, who choose to serve in uniform in the US Navy, become part of a profession with a rich and proud heritage.

FIGHTING THE BRITISH FOR INDEPENDENCE

"I have not yet begun to fight!"
—**Commodore John Paul Jones, during the heat of battle between the *Bonhomme Richard* and the HMS *Serapis*, when asked by the enemy if he was going to surrender**[1]

It was the evening of September 23, 1779, and the heated battle between the *Bonhomme Richard* and the HMS *Serapis* was not going well for Commodore John Paul Jones. In defiance of a direct order, he watched one of the ships under his command sail away from the battle, just as he was about to confront a convoy of British ships. Jones and his crew—a mix of Americans and British deserters—must have felt abandoned in their most dire time of need. Instead of retreating, Jones issued his famous response to the British.

The War of Independence

The colonies had made the bold decision to heighten the stakes in the war and take the fight directly to the enemy's own coastal waters. So, here was Jones, just off the coast of Scotland, poised and ready to attack. He was leading his squadron as commander of the *Bonhomme Richard*, a slow, aging vessel that was originally built as a merchant ship—not a warship. The *Bonhomme Richard* had made four trips back and forth to China by the time Jones acquired it. But Jones had done the best he could to make the old ship ready for battle on the high seas. And now it was going to be put to the ultimate test.

Captain Richard Pearson, a Royal Navy officer, commanded the lead ship in the British convoy, the HMS *Serapis*. He had more than thirty years of experience at sea. Jones rightly thought that capturing such a convoy right off the enemy coast would win the Americans a prize of naval supplies and would antagonize the British people. But Jones needed the help of the rest of his squadron. Pierre Landais, a French commander of the American frigate *Alliance*, was accompanying him, but he made it clear that he was not necessarily going to follow Jones's lead. When Jones gave the order to attack Pearson's convoy, Landais ignored him, sailing away and taking several other French vessels with him.

Frustrated with Landais, Jones decided to attack the *Serapis* alone. His crew fired the first shot, a broadside against Pearson's ship that started a fierce, close-range battle between the two ships—about twenty-five yards apart (a quarter of a football field). The *Bonhomme Richard* was no match for the *Serapis*, which was newer, faster, and better able to maneuver.

When two of the *Bonhomme Richard's* eighteen-pound guns exploded on the lower gun deck, the explosion instantly killed the gun crews and severely burned and otherwise wounded many more of the crewmembers.

The two ships continued to circle and engage each other. The *Bonhomme Richard* collided with the stern of the *Serapis*, leaving Jones and his crew helpless against the *Serapis's* after guns. Pearson shouted out to Jones, "Has your ship struck?" When a ship "strikes" its colors, it means the crew is surrendering and admitting defeat. Jones was defiant and yelled out the now famous words: "I have not yet begun to fight!"[2]

He meant it, for the battle continued for more than three hours. The *Bonhomme Richard's* crew was able to free their ship from the *Serapis's* stern and intentionally strike the *Serapis* again at a right angle, physically hooking the two ships together—like two bulls with locked horns.

Suddenly, the elusive and unpredictable Landais and his ship, the *Alliance*, reappeared—only to make the situation worse for Jones. It must have been a confusing and frightening sight for Landais and his crew to see the *Bonhomme Richard* and the *Serapis* hooked to each other, wading in thick smoke from the cannons and the small fires. In the chaos of the scene, the *Alliance* accidentally fired directly on the *Bonhomme Richard*! It was not until a frustrated Jones raised his recognition signal that the *Alliance* relented. (Jones believed the *Alliance's* attack had been deliberate, and he later filed charges against Landais, forcing his dismissal from the Navy.)

Larger, more threatening fires were breaking out on both ships, and the *Bonhomme Richard* appeared to be sinking. Just then, a huge explosion rocked the gun deck of the *Serapis*—

The 1779 battle between Commodore John Paul Jones's ship the *Bonhomme Richard* and Captain Richard Pearon's British frigate HMS *Serapis* is depicted in this engraving.

killing dozens of sailors and severely burning many others. What was the cause? A hand grenade had been lobbed onto the deck of the *Serapis* by one of Jones's sailors, setting off a series of explosions. This was the fatal blow for Pearson. As he saw his deck covered in blood and he glanced at the *Alliance* poised nearby to further inflict damage on his wounded and weary vessel, he surrendered.

The death toll from this battle was unusually high for battles in this era—more than 50 percent from each crew was lost. Despite the human losses, Jones's victory confirmed his heroic reputation and earned him a personal place in history as the "Father of the American Navy." But the battle success also established a new, winning reputation for the nation's young navy. This newfound respect was critical, for the United States had no national navy prior to the Revolutionary War.

Fighting Pirates

Terrorizing the Mediterranean in the early 1800s, pirates were loosely organized and not officially working for any particular government. But, they were causing physical damage to the ships they attacked, and they stole valuable goods intended for the free market. To protect the free passage of merchant ships throughout the world, the United States once again found itself at war.

After the Revolutionary War, the United States could not afford to keep the Continental Navy active, so Congress disposed of all the American warships.[3] But, when American merchants attempted to travel the globe in search of trade, they encountered a threat of a different kind. Routinely patrolling the Mediterranean Sea, rogue bands of pirates were

Beyond the Call of Duty: One Sailor's Initiative

William Hamilton, a sailor aboard the *Bonhomme Richard*, knew the HMS *Serapis* had superior firepower, but he also knew that Commodore Jones was wearing down the enemy's ability to fight with his steely resolve. So, Hamilton seized an opportunity to deliver the final blow when the two ships were entangled. He climbed out onto the yardarm with a basket of hand grenades and a live match, lit the fuse, and dropped a grenade right into an open hatch of the *Serapis*. It landed on some gunpowder that had been hastily left lying around. The explosions and fire that erupted killed more than twenty enemy men and seriously wounded many others. The captain of the *Serapis* had had enough—he surrendered to Jones on the spot.

not looking for control of land or people. They were looking for money. They wreaked havoc on American merchant ships that traveled by the Barbary States: Algiers, Tunis, Morocco, and Tripoli. They demanded payment or else they would take the crew and ship hostage—until a ransom was paid by the ship's host government.

One of those ships was the USS *Philadelphia*, which ran aground and was captured in the Tripoli harbor along with her crew in 1803. Negotiations were unsuccessful and the *Philadelphia* remained hostage—thousands of miles from home.

At the time, Lieutenant Stephen Decatur was a young naval officer, and he had a daring plan. Decatur decided to disguise a recently captured ship, the USS *Intrepid*, as a friendly vessel and sneak up for a surprise attack. On the evening of February 16, 1804, Decatur quietly sailed into the Tripoli harbor and nested next to the *Philadelphia*. His crew asked for an anchor line in Arabic, pretending that the *Intrepid* had lost its line. At close range, the Tripolitans recognized the foreigners and quickly alerted the rest of their crew, but Decatur and his small crew were still able to board the *Philadelphia*.

It took the Americans less than twenty minutes of brutal, hand-to-hand fighting with cutlasses and pikes—not a single gunshot was fired—to overpower the Tripolitans. With twenty enemy dead onboard, and the *Philadelphia*'s crew saved, Decatur's crew set the *Philadelphia* ablaze and—just as quickly—jumped back with the American crew from the *Philadelphia* onto the *Intrepid* and slid out of the harbor, as the *Philadelphia* burned to the waterline. Called the Battle of Tripoli, the surprise attack embarrassed the enemy, and it proved the Navy's ability—once again—to do more than just defend the American coastline. British admiral Horatio Nelson said the American raid on the Tripoli harbor was "the most bold and daring act of the age."[4]

The Second War of Independence

In the early 1800s, the British once again began to harass the United States. In its ongoing struggle for power in the world, Great Britain was taking notice of the United States' increase in international trade. Indeed, the United States' economy more than doubled between 1795 and 1806.[5]

The *Decatur* set the *Philadelphia* ablaze on Tripoli harbor.

The British decided to impose tariffs—or taxes—on the goods the United States attempted to ship through British ports, and British ships began to appear along the US eastern seaboard, taunting US merchant ships. President James Madison had had enough and asked Congress for a declaration of war against the British on June 1, 1812.

"Her Sides Are Made of Iron!"

So exclaimed a witness to the sea battle in 1812, upon watching the cannonballs literally "bounce" off the sides of the USS *Constitution*.[6]

Off the coast of Nova Scotia in August 1812 sat a shining example of American skill in shipbuilding: the USS *Constitution*. Its sides were reinforced with metal, making them particularly hard to penetrate. That day, the lookout noticed a British ship on the horizon. The *Constitution's* captain, Isaac Hull, immediately recognized the HMS *Guerrière*, as he knew James Dacres, the Guerrière's captain. The two of them had once shared a glass of wine and had waged a friendly bet over who would win in a ship-to-ship duel if they ever went to battle. They bet a hat.

Dacres believed his ship had faster firepower, and he mistakenly thought this would ensure his victory. But the *Constitution* maneuvered quite deftly and was able to dance around the Guerrière. When the British cannon shots did hit the *Constitution,* they appeared to bounce off the hull, earning the ship the nickname Old Ironsides. Instead, the *Constitution* struck the Guerrière repeatedly with devastating fire and was able to break the mizzenmast of the Guerrière with a few well-placed broadsides, completely disabling it. Dacres surrendered. Years later, he offered Hull his sword as a gesture of surrender. Hull took his hat instead.

This victory encouraged the Americans, who were suffering significant defeats in land battles during the War of 1812. It also shocked the British at home, who were overly confident that their naval superiority was assured.

"Don't Give Up the Ship!"

The border between Canada and the United States became hotly contested during the War of 1812. In fact, some Americans who supported this second war with the British were intent on conquering Canada. So, naval and army forces were sent to the Great Lakes region to mount invasions against our northern neighbors.

Master Commandant Oliver Hazard Perry took command of the American naval forces in Lake Erie in the

The USS *Constitution* earned the nickname "Old Ironsides" during the War of 1812.

spring of 1813 and quickly assembled a squadron of two twenty-gun brigs and nine smaller vessels and outfitted these ships with one hundred sharpshooters borrowed from the army.[7] He proceeded to stage his fleet in the western end of Lake Erie—antagonizing the British fleet and disrupting their control of the Lake.

With his supply lines in jeopardy, the British naval commander on scene, Captain Robert H. Barclay, had no choice but to engage Perry—despite being severely outweighed in firepower. The two fleets met on September 10, 1813. Perry's flagship, the USS *Lawrence*, took the lead and attacked the British at an acute angle to minimize the effect of the British gunfire. But the USS *Lawrence's* lead advantage turned into a disadvantage, as the rest of the squadron took too long to catch up. The USS *Lawrence* took the brunt of the casualties—with 80 percent of the crew killed or wounded. Realizing the *Lawrence* had little fight left in her, Perry had himself and a small crew rowed over to another ship in his squadron, the USS *Niagara*, to continue the battle. He maneuvered the USS *Niagara* across the bows of two of the British ships engaged with the USS *Lawrence*, ordered the remaining vessels in his fleet to back him up, and engaged the beleaguered British head on. They surrendered. With victory in his grasp, Perry penned a quick note to his superiors with the now famous quote that the enemy was now, indeed, under his control. It was a turning point in the war.

While this battle and other battles in the Great Lakes were small, they were some of the fiercest battles of the entire war. More important was their impact on the war's eventual outcome: American naval victories in the Great Lakes forced the British to give up their invasion of Ohio and allowed the US Army to take the offensive.

The war continued for two more years—with the Americans and British alternately gaining advantage. The British were unsuccessful in their attempts to gain control of the Great Lakes. They signed a peace treaty at the end of 1814 that effectively ended the War of 1812.

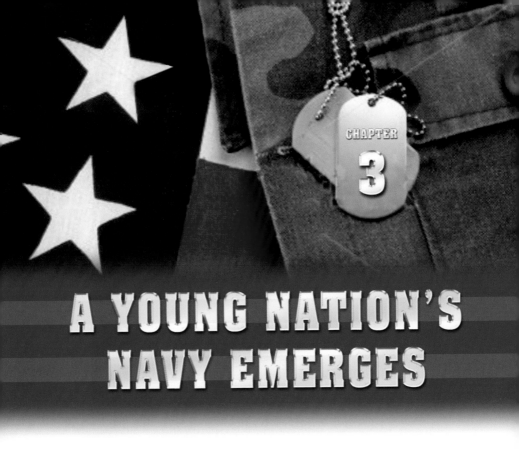

A YOUNG NATION'S NAVY EMERGES

Almost a century after the United States won its independence from Great Britain, the young nation was experiencing growing pains and the issue was once again the economy. Exploration and expansion westward were rapid, and more and more states were being added to the Union.

The economy of the southern states was dependent on agriculture and slaves provided the labor to produce these agricultural goods. When Abraham Lincoln—who many southerners thought would restrict or end slavery—was elected president, most southern states announced their secession from the rest of the country and formed the Confederacy. The nation went to war with itself and, while the war was mostly fought on land, there were some significant naval battles that tested the nation's fledgling navy.

Battle of the Ironclads

It looked "like a cheese box on a raft."
—A witness's reaction to seeing an
ironclad ship for the first time[1]

The sight of ships wrapped in iron—and floating—shocked the people who lived near the shores of the Chesapeake Bay in Hampton Roads, Virginia. It was the morning of March 9, 1862, and two most unusual ships were circling each other like rabid dogs. Bystanders (the battle was fought close to shore) were watching in awe. The two ships began firing at each other, and the battle between the CSS *Merrimack* and the USS *Monitor* had begun.

The Confederate secretary of the Navy, Stephen R. Mallory, was the force behind its first ironclad. He had seen the British and French prototypes. He convinced the Confederate navy to recover a partially burned hull of a steam frigate called the *Merrimack* and reconfigured it as an ironclad, covering it—like a fort—in plates of iron to protect it from cannonball fire. It was renamed the CSS *Virginia*.

Union spies reported that the Confederate navy was busy building a ship of the future that would repel enemy attacks. In response, the Union navy built its own.

It was designed by John Ericsson, an eccentric Union engineer who had the novel idea of building a ship entirely of iron and shaped more like a suboceanic species than a tall ship with sails. Many Union officials had doubts it could even float. Ericsson had studied the early experiments with ironclad ships. He had it built in one hundred days and incorporated the French and British designs with his own ideas. The result was radical and intimidating. And the USS *Monitor* sailed into the Chesapeake Bay harbor as a fierce opponent to the Confederate's *Virginia*.

The two ships accosted each other mid-morning and a circle dance ensued. The *Virginia*'s captain, Captain Franklin Buchanan, and the *Monitor*'s captain, Lieutenant John Worden, dueled for more than three hours—with little damage to either ship. As it turned out, the ironclads were quite resistant to attack, and both ships gave up midday. In effect, it was a draw.

While this particular battle produced no casualties, the ironclads proved their superiority to wooden ships. The technologies developed and tested during this war forever changed the way naval battles are fought. It signaled the beginning of the end of sail navies and the rest of the world took notice of this young nation.

Beyond the Call of Duty: One Sailor's Medal of Honor

As the helmsman of the USS *Monitor*, Quartermaster Peter Williams was under the direction of the captain of the ship, John Worden. But, when Worden was seriously wounded during the notorious Civil War duel and taken below decks for treatment, Williams successfully defended the ship on his own for several hours. For his bravery and successful maneuvering of the ship to avoid damage, he was awarded the Medal of Honor.

The battle between the two ironclads—the Union *Monitor* and the Confederate *Virginia*—resulted in a stalemate.

A Place to Train Naval Officers

For many years in the eighteenth century, Congress engaged in discussions about establishing a school for the preparation of naval officers for duty. There were many who believed that formal academic training had no value and that on-the-job training at sea was the only way to mold a formidable naval officer.

But the secretary of the Navy at the time, George Bancroft, believed a first-class navy needed a first-class school to train officers. He was successful in obtaining a piece of land on the Severn River in Annapolis, Maryland, from the Army. The United States Naval Academy was founded in 1845 with a handful of students. More than one hundred fifty years later, it is now a premier college with more than four thousand students. It sends approximately one thousand expertly trained Navy and Marine Corps officers to the fleet each year.

The US Navy Becomes a World Power

"What nation ever became a first-class power without a Navy?"

—Senator Samuel B. Maxey, Texas Democrat, in the late 1800s, as Congress debated the need for a bigger military.[2]

After the Civil War, the nation focused inward. Similar to most postwar periods in American history, the country reduced defense spending and let the military decline to a state of disrepair.[3]

In the late 1800s, the United States began to rebuild its Navy, as the country was industrializing and paying more and more attention to foreign markets. The United States wanted to increase the free trade of goods into and out of the country and wanted to protect US interests overseas. At the time, Theodore Roosevelt, the assistant secretary of the Navy, was heavily influenced by Captain Alfred Thayer Mahan, who advocated sea power and sea control as the means of establishing the United States as a world power in key areas of the world.[4]

"Remember the *Maine!*"

". . . ultimately those who wish to see this country at peace with foreign nations will be wise if they place reliance upon a first-class fleet of first-class battleships . . ."

—President Theodore Roosevelt, 1897 [5]

Designing a Ship That Goes Underwater

For centuries, inventors had toyed with the design of a ship that could navigate underwater, and American inventors were no different. Many of them tried to interest the US Navy in purchasing their designs. But it was not until someone thought of launching torpedoes from a submarine that the United States actually commissioned the production of one. A submarine was briefly used during the Civil War. It was designed by H.L. Hunley (and given the same name); it had mixed results.

John P. Holland built another submarine in 1897, the USS *Plunger*, which was eighty-five feet long and could carry two torpedoes. Holland's second, more improved submarine, could dive seventy-five feet and could maintain a surface speed of seven knots. He named this one after himself. Commodore George Dewey, victor at the Battle of Manila Bay, was impressed: "[If the Spaniards had] had two of these things in Manila, I could never have held it with the squadron I had."[6]

An officer sits in the *Plunger*'s conning tower hatch in the early 1900s.

When the battleship USS *Maine* was sunk by a surprise explosion off the coast of Cuba, Americans were outraged. The battle cry echoing throughout the halls of Congress was "Remember the *Maine*! To hell with Spain!" The United States had been conducting ongoing negotiations to purchase Cuba and the Philippines from Spain. Cubans had been revolting against Spanish control and the *Maine* was sent to Havana Harbor to protect Americans living there. On the evening of February 15, 1898, an explosion rocked the ship out of the water and destroyed its forward section. There were only 88 survivors out of a crew of 354 officers and enlisted. Two months later, the United States declared war on Spain. While the cause of the explosion was determined not to be sabotage, the sinking of the *Maine* was used by competing newspapers to lead the country into war. Because of public outcry after the media reports, the United States embarked on a war that proved its power and influence around the globe. The first fight of the war for the Navy was in Manila Bay, near the Spanish-dominated Philippines.

The assistant secretary of the Navy at the time, Theodore Roosevelt, appointed Commodore George Dewey as commander of the Asiatic Squadron. Dewey, a well-decorated veteran of the Civil War, had an aggressive reputation and was known for taking risks. Roosevelt had high hopes that Dewey would dominate the Spanish in the Philippines' Manila Bay.

Commodore Dewey was confident his heavy cruisers would outmaneuver the deteriorating Spanish fleet. However, he was worried about mines in Manila Bay, the shore support the Spanish fleet would have nearby, and the distance he would have to travel for repairs. (The closest friendly base was six hundred miles away in Hong Kong.)

In a devastating surprise attack, the USS *Maine* was destroyed in Havana Harbor. This event sparked the Spanish–American War.

Early in the morning of April 30, 1898, Dewey and his small fleet of warships quietly entered Manila Bay with little or no resistance. The Spanish fleet was ready, however, and once Dewey's fleet was inside the bay, the enemy began firing long before the American squadron was even in range. The Spanish fought heroically, but they were no match for the Americans. By lunchtime, most of the Spanish fleet was destroyed—with every vessel (except for two small launches) sinking or burning. In one day, Commodore Dewey had eliminated Spanish dominance from the Pacific.

American naval successes during the war also included the capture of Guam, a small Spanish-occupied island in

Led by Colonel Dewey, the USS *Olympia* defeated the Spanish fleet at the Battle of Manila Bay in the Philippines during the Spanish-American War.

the South Pacific. The Navy also successfully blockaded a Spanish fleet in Santiago Bay for over a month. Finally, the Spanish fleet steamed out of the bay, guns afire. The American ships destroyed every ship in the Spanish fleet. A little over a month later, Spain surrendered to the United States. American naval superiority around the world had been firmly established.

The Battleship Era

As an author of a naval history of the War of 1812 and a former assistant secretary of the Navy, President Teddy Roosevelt had been a strong advocate of the Navy as both a battle force and a strong show of power as a deterrent against potential enemies.

During his first term as president, Roosevelt doubled the Navy's budget and authorized the construction of numerous new ships. His favorite ship was the battleship. Battleships were large, wide, stocky vessels with tremendous fire-power—four twelve-inch guns for long-range reach (about nine miles), eight eight-inch guns for use at intermediate range, and twelve six-inch guns for use against short-range

President Roosevelt addressed the crew of the battleship USS *Connecticut* after the Great White Fleet of US Navy warships returned to Hampton Roads, Virginia.

targets (small boats). He took sixteen of them, painted them the peacetime color of white, and sent them on a round-the-world cruise to demonstrate to the world American technology and power. He called it the Great White Fleet and, although its mission was peaceful, there was no hiding the message: Don't mess with the United States!

US NAVY DEFENDS FREEDOM ALL OVER THE WORLD

The world wars of the twentieth century pitted many of the world's most powerful countries against each other. They brought violence and destruction on a scale the world had never seen before. The United States, which had been founded on the principles of freedom and independence, felt obligated to defend these principles on behalf of other countries. World Wars I and II, the Korean War, and the Vietnam War were all fought to prevent the spread of power by corrupt leaders and Communist governments throughout the world.

The First World War

It took several years before the United States got involved in World War I. The country was hesitant to get drawn into the ongoing bloody European struggle that had been waging for more than three years. But, American merchant ships traveling across the Atlantic were being threatened by the increasing presence of German U-boats—submarines that lurked beneath the surface and struck without warning, causing devastating effects. When a U-boat sank the cruise liner *Lusitania* in 1915, it killed 1,198 people, including 128 Americans.[1]

Safety in Numbers: Convoy Escorts

Rear Admiral William S. Sims was shocked. As a special envoy to the Royal Navy in April 1917, he was dumbfounded to learn that the British were suffering badly at the hands of the Germans. Sims and most of the American people assumed U-boat attacks were a nuisance to the British, but they had no idea the British were losing the war.

Sims, known for his eagerness to try new ideas in the Navy, was sold on the Royal Navy's idea of convoys. Based on the theory of "safety in numbers," the strategy of using warships to physically escort a large group of merchant ships was a controversial one. Some military planners at the time thought it made the merchant ships and warships even more vulnerable—as a large group of ships traveling together would be even easier to find and target for attack. Some merchant-ship captains feared collisions from so many ships traveling so closely together. But a study of shipping records showed that merchant ships traveling together had a better survival rate.[2] So, the United States decided to try it.

It worked. When the ships began to travel in convoys during the summer of 1917, merchant-ship sinkings and losses dropped dramatically: from 20 percent to 0.5 percent over the next few months.[3]

World War I officially ended on November 11, 1918, a day that was named Armistice Day, and is now annually celebrated in the United States as Veterans Day. During this "Great War," which lasted four years, Germany and its allies—the Central Powers—were defeated. However, the war left Great Britain and France impoverished, and it had plunged Russia into a revolution. The social and political order of the entire continent was disrupted, setting the stage for the rise of fascism in Italy and Nazism in Germany.[4]

Launching a Plane From the Deck of a Ship

Innovative naval architects had been tinkering with the idea of launching a plane off the deck of a ship for some time, most notably a civilian professor named Samuel P. Langley. It made tactical sense—an aviator would be a much better enemy scout than any individual on a ship could be. Eugene Ely completed the first successful takeoff from a ship in 1910. He landed on a beach nearby. It was not until 1920 that a ship was actually designed for planes to take off and land. Named after the man who conceived the idea, the USS *Langley* was an old collier (cargo ship) that workmen stripped down topside and refitted with a 534-foot-long deck.

The Second World War

Without victory in World War II by the United States and the Allies, the world would be a different place today. Adolf Hitler's rise to power in Germany in the 1930s and his coalition of fascist countries, including Italy and Japan, were threatening democracies and freedoms all over the world. But it was not until an attack on US soil destroyed a large portion of its Navy in port that the United States formally joined the Allies in battle.

In the first successful takeoff from a ship deck, Eugene Ely took off in a 50-horsepower Curtiss plane from a wooden platform built over the bow of the light cruiser USS *Birmingham* in 1910.

December 7, 1941

> *"... a date that will live in infamy ..."*
> —President Franklin D. Roosevelt,
>   in a speech to the American people,
>   describing the devastation of the
>   Pearl Harbor attacks[5]

That Sunday morning in Pearl Harbor, Hawaii, started out peacefully. The tropical harbor near Honolulu was not considered a war zone, but a logical place to stage US Pacific

Fleet forces, as it was part way between the US West Coast and Asia.

It was Sunday morning, and Ship's Cook Third Class Doris "Dorie" Miller was attending to his early morning duties on the mess deck of the USS *West Virginia*. He was big and strong, so he was doubly assigned as an ammunition handler in the antiaircraft battery magazine—although he had never fired the guns himself. But, this morning, December 7, 1941, was different. The US ships were extremely vulnerable. The Japanese had assembled their best attack airplanes, launched them from aircraft carriers, and attacked the US Navy on its own shores.

The effect was devastating. Five battleships were sunk and three more were severely disabled. It took the group effort of every survivor to save the wounded sailors and the sinking ships.

The USS *West Virginia* and other ships moored in the harbor were hit hard; some sank to the bottom of the harbor and some were close to sinking. The patience, skills, and physical and inner strength of Miller became critical. He hauled numerous wounded shipmates from below decks in search of medical treatment, and then he manned an antiaircraft machine gun and proceeded to fire on Japanese aircraft. Where had he acquired this expertise? "It wasn't hard. I just pulled the trigger and she worked fine. I had watched the others with these guns. I guess I fired her for about 15 minutes."[6]

Miller was awarded the Navy's second highest award, the Navy Cross, by Admiral Chester Nimitz, commander in chief of the Pacific Fleet. Miller was the first African American to receive such an honor.

The USS *West Virginia* was hit hard during the attack on Pearl Harbor.

Turning the Tide of the War in the Pacific

The Japanese were in a hurry. At the time of the Pearl Harbor attack, the Japanese were enjoying naval superiority in the Pacific, but they knew it would not last long, as the United States was mobilizing quickly for war. The Japanese wanted more territory and they also wanted to destroy American aircraft carriers, which were out to sea during the attack on Pearl Harbor. The Japanese set their sights on a small island called Midway and planned an aggressive attack. Their plan was to lure the United States' aircraft carriers into a trap.

However, American codebreakers were able to decipher the date and location of the attack, eliminating the element of surprise and giving them time for the US Navy to prepare its own ambush. While the Japanese carpet-bombed the island of Midway early on the morning of June 4, 1942, with little or no resistance, American ships snuck up on the Japanese carriers to launch a surprise counterattack.

Tragically, the first squadron of US torpedo bombers who found the Japanese carriers was devastated—with 35 of the 41 planes shot down by the Japanese fighters and not a single Japanese plane hit. But this early setback had a positive result. To attack American bombers, the Japanese fighters had dipped down to a vulnerably low height. When American dive bombers arrived on the scene, they found the Japanese carriers littered with flammable debris hastily left on the decks and exposed with no jet protection. The dive bombers moved in for the attack and quickly sank three of the four Japanese carriers. The Japanese valiantly fought back, but America won the last round—finishing off the fourth Japanese carrier, the *Hiryu*, late that afternoon.

The entire Japanese carrier force had been destroyed in one day and this ended a six-month string of Japanese victories. The US Navy was victorious and the tide had turned in the Pacific Campaign of World War II.

The Cold War: Fighting the Spread of Communism

After the United States and its Allies defeated Hitler and ended World War II, the Soviet Union became determined to spread communism around the world. Two areas that became of particular concern to the United States were Korea and Vietnam. The Communists and their handpicked North

US Navy torpedo bombers soar over a burning Japanese ship during the Battle of Midway.

Korean and North Vietnamese leaders dug in and began to exert their power and influence over the governments in each country. Then the Communists attempted to invade the southern half of each country, increasing the fear that the Soviets and their Communist allies wanted to dominate the world, one country at a time.

War at the Thirty-Eighth Parallel

When North Korea, led by its Communist and Soviet-backed leader Kim Il Sung, crossed the 38th parallel (referring to a latitude on Earth's Northern Hemisphere) and invaded South Korea on June 25, 1950, the United Nations voted to repel the attack. The United States immediately sent ground, naval, and air units to support the South Koreans. Naval and air forces began attacking the North Koreans with bombs dropped from planes and with guns from Navy cruisers and destroyers. The American ground forces also fought against the North Korean aggressors.

These efforts stabilized the situation in South Korea, preventing the North Koreans from moving farther south. However, they did not retreat. So, the United States government determined that an amphibious landing with ground forces was necessary—behind enemy lines.

The Landing at Inchon

"The Navy and Marines have never shone so brightly than this morning."
—General Douglas MacArthur, the lead Army general during the Korean conflict, describing the actions of the US Navy and Marine Corps at Inchon.[7]

Rear Admiral James P. Doyle was in a difficult situation. He was tasked with staging the largest amphibious assault since the end of World War II. But, the United States had decommissioned hundreds of its warships after World War II, in order to focus on rebuilding the American economy during peacetime. By 1950, the United States had a much smaller Navy, and the ships still in operation were old.

Nonetheless, Rear Admiral Doyle successfully assembled a multinational fleet of several hundred ships. It descended on the western coast of Korea for a showdown with North Korea and its Communist backers. The geography surrounding Inchon made it very difficult—almost inaccessible—for an amphibious landing. It had one of the largest tidal ranges—more than thirty-one feet—in any given day and was filled with outlying reefs, small islands, and shoals. The currents shifted quickly as the tides changed. Once ashore, the mudflats and ensuing seawalls would be daunting to Marines racing to fight the enemy through an industrial city the size of Omaha, Nebraska.

So, after three days of "softening" up the shore with air strikes, the convoy of ships inched their way up the narrow channel toward the coast at Inchon on the morning of September 15, 1950. Carefully navigating the obstacle course without the benefit of practice, the fleet landed an advance regiment of Marines who hoisted an American flag at the top of a hill. By dawn the next morning, the American forces had taken the city of Inchon and were moving toward Seoul. The American flag was raised in Seoul twelve days later, on September 27. The landing at Inchon was victorious, and it showed how flexible the Navy could be in responding quickly and aggressively to threats anywhere in the world.

It would take almost three more years of fighting before an armistice was signed on July 27, 1953, officially ending the conflict. The agreement created the Korean Demilitarized Zone (DMZ) to separate North and South Korea. Tensions between the two countries remain high to this day and the United States maintains a presence at the DMZ to protect South Korea.

"Underway on Nuclear Power"

When the USS *Nautilus* went to sea under nuclear power from Groton, Connecticut, on September 30, 1954, it was a national milestone. The development of nuclear power and its use to propel submarines is one of the most significant technological developments of the Cold War. The maiden voyage of the USS *Nautilus*, the first nuclear-powered submarine, made submarines truly "submersible." They could now remain underwater without refueling for long periods of time.

The driving force behind this technological innovation was Admiral Hyman G. Rickover, a naval officer who was the leading expert on nuclear propulsion. He had a difficult personality and was not well liked. Many inside and outside the Navy despised him personally, but they could not deny his genius and dedicated advocacy of the strategic and national advantage of nuclear power. When the *Nautilus* left the port of Groton, Commander Eugene Wilkinson, the *Nautilus* commanding officer, reported—for the first time—"Underway on nuclear power."

The Vietnam War

With the end of the Korean War in 1953, the Communists turned their attention to Vietnam. The Vietnamese

Communists were successful in repelling the French from their country in 1954, ending more than a century of colonization. They then consolidated Communist power in northern Vietnam, splitting the country in two. The United States began to send supplies and military advisers to South Vietnam to prevent the spread of communism southward.

The North Vietnamese had a very small navy, so US aircraft carriers, destroyers, and cruisers spent a great deal of time cruising the thousand-mile coastline of Vietnam.[8] In addition, the United States patrolled the four-thousand-mile system of rivers, canals, and estuaries (small bays) in the Mekong Delta area of South Vietnam. Using small riverine vessels in these waterways, the Navy inspected small boats to ensure they were legitimate commercial traffic and not hiding enemy forces. It also operated a variety of other small craft in the rivers and worked closely with the US Army and South Vietnamese forces.

These fleets of river patrol boats (PBRs) were the workhorses of the Navy in these dangerous, shallow waters. Their mission was to knock out guerilla positions hidden in the jungle and serve as escorts for larger amphibious ships, protecting them from guerillas and floating mines. These boats were dark green and just thirty-one feet long. Instead of propellers, they had a water jet system, which enabled them to navigate in very shallow waters.[9] Each PBR was manned by a crew of four or five men and was armed with machine guns and grenade launchers. Army and Navy helicopters provided air support.

One of the largest firefights involving PBRs took place on October 31, 1966. Boatswain's Mate First Class James Williams was in charge of two PBR crews and stumbled upon

Beyond the Call of Duty: A Sailor Saves Lives as a POW

Seaman Apprentice Doug Hegdahl did not expect to run into any danger as a young Navy sailor, and he certainly did not expect to be treading water in the black of night as a type of Vietnam War castaway. On the contrary, Hegdahl expected to do his time on board his ship, see the world, and then go back home to South Dakota.

While on station in the Gulf of Tonkin as a crewmember of the USS *Canberra* on the night of April 6, 1967, Hegdahl wanted to witness some of the nighttime attacks that were being waged from his ship. He was warned of the danger of venturing onto the decks of his ship during the nighttime shelling, but the possibility of seeing a fireworks display was too tempting.

The blast of the five-inch guns above him blew Hegdahl overboard. He was picked up by the North Vietnamese and held as a prisoner of war (POW) for more than two years. His life in the prison camp was one of hardship, but some of his fellow prisoners noticed that Hegdahl had an unusually good memory. His POW roommate, Captain Dick Stratton, said, "When I first met him, he asked me if I knew the Gettysburg Address and we got a rock and wrote it on the floor and he could say it backward. Now, why you'd want to say it backward, I don't know, but he could."

Hegdahl reminisces, "I'd always memorized lists of presidents and state capitals—which is kinda trivia. So, why not take that ability and harness it for something practical like memorizing names of POWs or camp locations. Eventually, I memorized 250." When he was released in August 1969, his memory gave peace of mind to 250 families who did not know if their loved one was alive or dead.[10]

Botswain's Mate First Class James Williams (pictured in white uniform) received the prestigious Medal of Honor from President Lyndon Johnson (right) for his heroism during the Vietnam War.

---

enemy forces hiding in several junk boats floating ahead of him. The men on deck were wearing North Vietnamese military uniforms, so it was obvious to the PBR crews that these unidentified vessels were *not* commercial.[11] Williams and his two boat crews chased and destroyed the two enemy boats. In their hot pursuit down a narrow canal, they suddenly came upon a fleet of forty to fifty more boats, all heavily laden with men and weapons. With little time to react, Williams decided to bombard the junk boats head on.

As he described in an interview later in his southern accent, "Ya'll got to understand. There weren't no exit ramp."[12] Williams and his two PBRs actually ran right over several small enemy boats—crushing many of the flimsy structures and leaving the surprised enemies bobbing in the water. Williams and his crews emerged almost completely unscathed. He immediately called in for helicopter support, then turned around and, once again, charged into the enemy fleet. His two boats and the helicopters destroyed more than fifty enemy vessels and they captured a half dozen more.[13] Williams was awarded the Medal of Honor for his heroic efforts that day.

Chasing Soviet Submarines

The Navy played a critical role in the Cold War—in Korea, Vietnam, and in the silent wars waged underwater between American and Soviet submarines. It was a game of cat and mouse, with each country's vessels creeping around each other quietly, deep in the ocean—sometimes right under the other's nose.

As described in the book *Blind Man's Bluff*:

No other intelligence operation has embraced so many generations of a single military force, no other has consistently placed so many Americans at risk. As many as 140 men on each sub, several subs at a time, nearly every man who ever served on a US attack submarine was sent to watch Soviet harbors and shipyards, monitor Soviet missile tests, or shadow Soviet subs.[14]

It was a lonely job at the forefront of the Cold War, and the Navy men who volunteered for submarine duty spent many months away from home *and* beneath the surface of the ocean. But their sacrifice played a critical role in enhancing

The nuclear ballistic missile submarine USS *George Washington* patrolled the Atlantic and Pacific oceans for 25 years.

the United States' knowledge of the Soviets' military capability, which, in turn, enabled the United States to deter and anticipate any attack.

War in the Middle East: Operation Desert Storm

Since the end of the Cold War, the US military has turned its focus to the Middle East. When Saddam Hussein, Iraqi political leader, sanctioned an Iraqi invasion of the neighboring country of Kuwait in August 1990, the entire world—led by the United States—was determined to help the Kuwaitis. A coalition of forces from countries all over the world sent almost five hundred thousand servicemen and women to repel Saddam Hussein. The Navy transported many of these troops and their equipment, bombed military targets in

Tomawhawk Cruise Missiles Hit Their Mark

The USS *Louisville* (SSN-724), a Los Angeles class fast-attack submarine, made naval history in 1991 when it fired the first submarine-launched Tomahawk cruise missile in war. A Tomahawk guided cruise missile is powered by a jet engine and is designed to attack a variety of surface targets. It can carry a wide variety of warhead, guidance, and range capabilities. With a crew of 127 men, the *Louisville* made a high-speed voyage across the Pacific and Indian Oceans to the Red Sea—traveling fourteen thousand miles under-water—to arrive on station in time for battle and for the successful launch. The ship and crew were awarded the Navy Unit Commendation for their exceptional meritorious service.[15]

The international coalition was successful in defeating Saddam Hussein. He surrendered, retreated back to Iraq, and Kuwait was once again a free and independent country. The US Navy had once again played a critical role in providing sustained air power and shore bombardment without the use of a land base. However, it was not until twelve years later that Saddam Hussein was removed from power.

Iraq, and patrolled the Persian Gulf. Maritime superiority remained critical—both to cut off Saddam Hussein's supply lines and to protect American supply lines and vital oil platforms.

After several weeks of a relentless air offensive, the international coalition launched an attack against the Iraqi forces in Kuwait and Iraq. In the first 24 hours of the war, the United States flew 1,400 sorties and American ships and submarines fired 104 Tomahawk missiles.[16]

The naval air power used in Operation Desert Storm was awe-inspiring. Navy aircraft from four aircraft carrier battle groups struck targets up to seven hundred miles away—destroying Iraq's air and naval forces, anti-air defense, ballistic missile launchers, communications networks, and electrical power grids.[17] In addition, shore-based Navy P-3 Orion and S-3 aircraft patrolled the shipping lanes in the Persian Gulf. Helicopters performed search and rescue missions, medical evacuation, and logistics.

NAVAL OPERATIONS TODAY

On September 11, 2001, Americans woke up to multiple devastating attacks on our country. Planes flew into the World Trade Center twin towers in in New York City and the Pentagon in Washington, D.C., toppling the towers and inflicting significant structural damage to the Pentagon. A total of 2,996 people were killed that day and the events changed the United States forever.

The Global War on Terrorism was launched and more than fourteen years later, the Navy continues to play a critical role—conducting air attacks in Iraq and Afghanistan, patrolling the ocean and seas of the region, fighting insurgents with Navy SEALs, providing medical care with Navy doctors, nurses and hospital corpsmen, and building infrastructure with Navy construction battalions.

Those who choose to join and serve in the US Navy today can expect more time at sea, which means more time

Navy SEALs Execute Osama bin Laden

On a warm night in May 2011 with little moonlight, two small teams of Navy SEALs from the Naval Special Warfare Development Group (or DEVGRU) flew over the border from Afghanistan to Pakistan in two CH-47 Chinook helicopters. The men didn't talk much. They knew their mission, Operation Neptune Spear, was going to require all their concentration, energy, training, and expertise. They also knew that the mission was extremely dangerous and they might die in the attempt. They were on their way to a raid on Osama bin Laden's hideout.

The mastermind behind the September 11, 2001, attacks on the World Trade Center and the Pentagon, bin Laden had been on the hit list of the United States ever since. Now, the military and the Central Intelligence Agency (CIA) were confident they had found him. Quietly inserted into a residential compound in Abbottabad and wearing night-vision goggles, the SEALs quickly entered the house, not knowing how many people they would encounter and how heavily armed they would be. They searched room by room and finally found bin Laden on the third floor hiding behind his wife, where they instantly killed him with rifles customized for just such a mission. They took his body with them and jumped back on their helicopters and flew back to Afghanistan. The entire mission took 38 minutes.

away from family and friends. That is the reality. However, serving one's nation and helping the cause of freedom around the world is an intangible reward that cannot be measured.

"Where Are the Carriers?"

Nothing symbolizes the power and strength of the Navy like an aircraft carrier. The United States has invested a lot of money and technology into the building and maintenance of its fleet of aircraft carriers. Aircraft carriers are a daunting sight on the horizon. They serve both as platforms for sending firepower to the enemy and as a strong deterrent of conflict.

"Where are the carriers?" US presidents frequently ask this question of their military leaders when faced with an international crisis. They rely on the centerpiece of the US Navy—the fleet of aircraft carriers—to deter current and potential enemies of the United States. The nation's leaders rely on these gigantic, floating airports to support and operate aircraft that engage in attack, surveillance, and electronic warfare against targets at sea, in the air, or ashore.[1] These 91,400-ton ships lead a "battle group" of military might that includes cruisers, destroyers, submarines, and frigates, plus several squadrons of aircraft. This collection of firepower lingers off the shores of foreign countries, and sends a clear message to enemies of the United States.

What is it like to work on an aircraft carrier today? At sea on the USS *George Washington*, the days are long and the pace is fast. The center of activity is the flight deck—a small airport and landing strip that can "launch" a plane every forty-five seconds. When the ship is at sea, the sailors assigned to the flight deck scurry around almost twenty-four hours a

The USS *George Washington* is also the name of a nuclear-powered aircraft carrier.

day in their purple, green, yellow, white, and brown-colored shirts. Each shirt color identifies a different job on board this massive, floating city.

The flight deck crew is all part of a well-coordinated "ballet," a detailed series of directions to move the maximum number of planes on and off the deck in the shortest amount of time possible.

Lieutenant Commander David Larsen is one of the USS *George Washington*'s catapult officers. He launches and helps land different types of aircraft. An aviator himself, Lieutenant Commander Larsen is responsible for the *George Washington*'s catapults—slingshots that can propel a thirty-six-ton aircraft off the bow of the ship into the air. The *George Washington* has a total of four catapults on board.

When the planes finish their mission and fly back to the ship, they lower their "tail hook," a big metal hook that is attached to the underside of the aircraft. As they approach the flight deck of the carrier, they scoop the hook under an arresting wire, a large wire—like a rubber band—that is stretched taut across the width of the ship. This wire stops the aircraft in two hundred feet—which is a much shorter distance than a commercial runway.

The *George Washington* is 1,092 feet long (a football field is 300 feet long), 257 feet wide, 244 feet high, weighs 97,000 tons, has a crew of more than 5,000 sailors and aviators, and carries 85 aircraft aboard. The ship serves more than eighteen thousand meals each day while underway at sea and has a distilling plant that can process four hundred thousand gallons of fresh water each day. It is truly a small city, with chaplains, doctors, dentists, pilots, lawyers, plumbers, mechanics, chemists, weather forecasters, air traffic controllers, security

As the USS *George Washington* sails in the Persian Gulf, an F/A-18 Hornet takes off while the other aircraft wait in line.

guards, journalists, photographers, barbers, cooks, and a host of other specialists—all living together on board. When these men and women deploy, they leave their families for six or more months at a time.

While aircraft carriers and the ships, submarines, and aircraft that accompany them focus on protecting the seas and sending air power ashore, the US Navy performs many other missions to protect the nation from harm.

Navy Humanitarian Relief Efforts

In recent years, the US Navy has played a role in world relief efforts. This has included the effects of the 2004 tsunami in Indonesia, Hurricane Katrina on the Gulf Coast in 2005, and the 2010 earthquake in Haiti.

Crew members from the aircraft carrier USS *Abraham Lincoln* worked around the clock in the Aceh Province, Sumatra, Indonesia, ensuring that vital food, water, and medical supplies were carried to survivors of the 2004 tsunami. They used the ship's trucks, helicopters, and hands to get the supplies from the coast deep into isolated villages and towns. Machinist's Mate First Class William Gregory, of Redding, California, said, "It makes me feel like I did something good for my country and for this country."[2]

When Hurricane Katrina devastated New Orleans, the USS *Iwo Jima* pulled into port soon after the storm subsided

Following the 2004 tsunami, US forces assisted victims in Indonesia. Here, military personnel carry a patient to a US Navy MH-60S Seahawk helicopter for a medical evacuation flight to the Military Sealift Command hospital ship USNS *Mercy* for treatment.

During Hurricane Katrina, the USS *Iwo Jima* served as a base on the Gulf Coast for rescue helicopters.

and became a center for relief efforts. As the commanding officer, Captain Richard Callas, relayed in an e-mail dated September 12, 2005:

> *Within the first 24 hours after arriving pier side in New Orleans, the* Iwo Jima *has become many things. We are one of the few full service airports in the area and have been operating aircraft on and off our [flight] deck for almost 15 hours each day. We are also one of the only air-conditioned facilities within a ten-mile radius and, though we have had problems making water from the polluted Mississippi [River], we are also the only hot shower within miles. All day long, we have been accommodating local policemen, firemen, state troopers, National Guard, [and] the 82nd airborne division personnel with hot showers and hot food.*[3]

When a 7.0 earthquake hit the island nation of Haiti on January 12, 2010, the devastation was catastrophic. The Navy responded immediately with more than 10,000 Sailors and Marines, 17 ships, 48 helicopters, and 12 fixed-wing aircraft —delivering relief supplies for distribution to affected areas. In addition, the hospital ship USNS *Comfort* was sent with the supplies, facilities, and skilled medical personnel equivalent to a complete hospital.

The Navy's Expanding Roles

In addition to the traditional ocean-based warfare, the Navy has deployed riverine warfare units to will be responsible for inserting and extracting special operations personnel. They will also conduct fire support and provide security along an enemy's coast.[4]

After an earthquake devastated Haiti, US military personnel were deployed to the island to help. Here, army and navy soldiers work together unloading food and supplies for the many victims.

At the same time, the Navy has greatly expanded the SEALs' and special operations' role in the war on terrorism in Iraq and Afghanistan. "Special operations teams are covering the gamut of warfare, from direct-action missions to hunt and seize terrorists to . . . providing medical care," says Vice Admiral Eric Olson, former commander of Special Operations Command.[5]

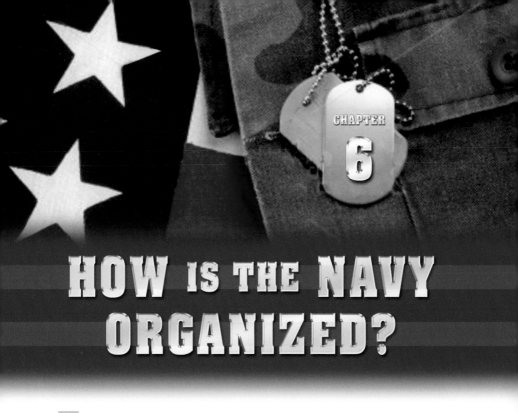

HOW IS THE NAVY ORGANIZED?

The United States has designed its military services so that civilians always oversee it. This ensures that a military dictator can never take control of the civilian population. Visually, the organizational relationship between the president of the United States and the Navy is shaped like a pyramid, with the president at the top. He assumes the title commander-in-chief when he makes military decisions.

Directly reporting to him is the Secretary of Defense, who is appointed by the president and is a civilian. The Secretary of Defense acts as a type of chief executive officer of all the services: the Army, the Air Force, the Coast Guard, and the Marine Corps. Reporting to him is the Secretary of the Navy, also a civilian and also appointed by the president, who oversees the Navy and the Marine Corps. Reporting to him is the Navy's top-ranked, uniformed person is called the chief of naval operations, or CNO, a four-star admiral.

The secretary of the Navy, the Honorable Dr. Donald C. Winter (center); chief of naval operations, Admiral Mike Mullen (left); and the master chief petty officer of the Navy, Terry Scott, pose for a photo at the Pentagon in January 2006.

The Joint Chiefs of Staff

The National Security Act of 1947 created the joint chiefs of staff (JCS)—out of a need for a more formal joint command structure. As a member of the JCS, the CNO is the president's and the Secretary of Defense's primary adviser on the conduct of naval warfare. He or she is also the principal administrative adviser to the secretary of the Navy.[1]

The United States military is divided into several geographically based commands: US Northern Command, US Pacific Command, US Southern Command, US Central Command, and the US European Command. Each one of these commands includes fleets of ships, aircraft, submarines, bases, and sailors. When the Navy goes to sea around the world, it usually travels in groups of ships, aircraft, and submarines.

Aircraft Carrier Strike Groups

Aircraft carriers are the centerpiece of a "carrier strike group," a group of ships that travels together in support of American foreign policy abroad. In addition to an aircraft carrier, the strike group usually includes cruisers—surface ships used primarily for anti-air warfare—and destroyers and frigates—surface ships used primarily for antisubmarine warfare. It also includes a fast-attack submarine, used primarily to seek out

The USS *George Washington* sails in a carrier strike group formation on the Atlantic Ocean.

A close-up of a US Navy strike group shows the guided missile cruiser USS *Monterey*, guided missile destroyer USS *Stout* and guided missile frigate USS *Underwood* as they prepare to pull alongside Nimitz-class aircraft carrier USS *George Washington*.

and destroy hostile surface ships; other submarines; and a supply ship that carries ammunition, oil, and other supplies.

In addition, the aircraft carrier hosts a carrier air wing. With up to eighty aircraft, the air wing includes fighter aircraft, attack aircraft, antisubmarine war fighting aircraft (both jets and helicopters), surveillance aircraft, and cargo aircraft.

In addition to carrier strike groups, the US Navy also uses an expeditionary strike group (ESG) to support its mission overseas. This consists of strike-capable surface warships and submarines, which are increasingly being used in areas of smaller threats. These warships typically include amphibious ships (to carry and deliver marines and helicopters to shore), a cruiser, a destroyer, frigates, and a submarine.

Navy Ranks

Within each one of these ships is a crew that is made up of both officers and enlisted sailors who work closely together to make the ship run smoothly. The current active naval force consists of approximately 325,000 people.[2] Of those individuals, approximately 267,100 are enlisted sailors who join the Navy right out of high school (or who are older, but do not have a college degree). A total of approximately 53,500 officers currently serve on active duty at any time. They are required to have a college degree, and they are responsible for supervising the enlisted sailors. A junior-grade lieutenant officer who has only one to four years of experience in the Navy could be responsible for overseeing several dozen enlisted men and women.

When Navy ships are docked in port at bases around the world, the bases provide the maintenance and support for the

Officers and crew of the amphibious assault ship USS *Essex* line the rails as the ship returns after completing a two-month deployment partrolling several Southeast Asian countries.

ships and the crews. Naval bases have repair and maintenance facilities, office buildings for support staff, and housing for the crews' families.

In the past, naval crews consisted of only men. However, today women make up part of the diverse American naval force.

DIVERSITY IN THE NAVY

American women have been serving honorably in the nation's armed forces—and the Navy—since its creation. Women worked on ships of all types in the seventeenth and eighteenth centuries, including hospital ships, whaling ships, merchant ships, pirate and privateer ships, clipper ships, and warships.[1]

But in 2013 then-Secretary of Defense Leon Panetta announced a groundbreaking decision to overturn a 1994 rule that restricted women from artillery, armor, infantry and other such combat roles, opening up hundreds of thousands of frontline positions that women had previously been barred from performing.

Women in the Navy

American women distinguished themselves in the Revolutionary and Civil wars as nurses and surgical

Wendy Lawrence:
Naval Officer and Astronaut

As a member of one of the first classes at the US Naval Academy to include women, Captain Wendy Lawrence is a trailblazer. She became a naval aviator and logged more than 1,500 hours of flight time in six different helicopters and more than eight hundred ship landings. She was selected in 1992 by NASA to be an astronaut and logged more than 1,225 hours in space, including aboard the STS-114 *Discovery* flight in July 2005.

assistants. They cared for combat wounded and ran military hospitals. In 1908, Congress authorized the Navy Nurse Corps, formally establishing roles for American women nurses in the Navy to serve around the country and overseas.

When the United States entered World War I, there was a severe manpower shortage, so women were recruited for additional jobs. In addition to expanded roles in nursing, they worked as "yeomanettes" and Marine Reservists, providing administrative and clerical support. It was certainly considered an unusual step for women to take at the time, but their patriotism and desire to help their country obviously played a role in their decision.

When World War II broke out, all the military services were looking for people to cover the jobs left by men sent overseas to fight the Germans and the Japanese. So, the armed forces increasingly turned to women. The United States created Women Accepted for Voluntary Emergency Services (WAVES) and some three hundred fifty thousand women stepped up to the job.[2]

After World War II, the number of women in the Navy and the types of jobs they performed actually decreased. Their role in the postwar world was more commonly in the home—as wives and mothers. But, the conflicts in Korea and Vietnam once again called for the expertise and experience of Navy nurses, who were sent to war zones in increasing numbers. It was not until the early 1970s that women were allowed to venture onto ships and aircraft as crew members. The feminism that was sweeping the country fueled the demand to put women in jobs that were previously unavailable to them. This led to the end of the WAVES and the full integration of women into the US Navy.

During World War II, women were accepted into the navy as WAVES. Just one year after their admittance 27,000 women wore the WAVES uniform.

Since the 1970s, women have rapidly assumed jobs in almost every community in the US Navy:

◆ Women entered the US Naval Academy for the first time in 1976.

◆ Women were allowed to enter aviation training to fly naval aircraft with the first graduate, Lieutenant Barbara Allen, qualifying in 1974. They were allowed to fly combat aircraft and to be permanently assigned to aircraft carriers for the first time in 1994.

◆ Women have served on ships since 1972 and have served on warships since 1992. The first woman to command a Navy warship was Captain Kathleen McGrath. She took command of the USS *Jarrett* in 2000.

In 2010, the Department of the Navy changed its policy and began to allow qualified women to serve on submarines. The first group of nuclear-trained women officers started serving on ballistic missile submarines—larger than fast attack submarines—in 2011. In January 2015, the first group of women reported aboard the fast attack submarine USS *Minnesota*. Enlisted women are scheduled to first report for duty on submarines in 2016.

Operations Desert Shield and Desert Storm led to a wide-scale deployment of more than five hundred thousand servicemen and women to the Persian Gulf to repel Saddam Hussein from Kuwait. Navy women served in a variety of roles: on ammunition and supply ships, on helicopters, in construction jobs, and at fleet hospitals as doctors, nurses, and corpsmen. The women served admirably and honorably.

Soon afterward, women were given the opportunity to pilot combat airplanes, serve on combat ships and submarines. There is speculation that special operations positions will also be opened to women. Many of these changes is due to the Global War on Terrorism, and the difference in how "frontlines" and "combat" are defined. Supply lines and hospital tents are just as vulnerable to attack as a tank convoy, and many Navy women serving in noncombat jobs have been injured and killed in action.

Minorities' Contributions to the Navy

Minorities today will find the armed forces to be one of the most integrated organizations in the country and the Navy is no exception. But this was not always the case.

While African Americans have always served in the Navy, they were initially relegated to the galleys (kitchens) and the

Aviation Boatswains Mate Airman Raynelle Brown attaches a fuel nozzle to an SH-60F Seahawk helicopter from aboard nuclear-powered aircraft carrier USS *Nimitz*.

engine rooms. Racism prevented them from serving alongside white sailors. When they were allowed to fight, it was in segregated units. After World War II, however, Congress changed the laws to allow all servicemen (and women)—regardless of race—to serve in regular, integrated units. Since then, minorities have increasingly served in all ranks and designations.

Among the highlights in African-American US naval history are:

♦ Thirteen African Americans were commissioned as officers in the US Navy for the first time in March 1944.

♦ Ensign Jesse LeRoy Brown became the first African-American naval aviator when he received his wings of gold in 1948.

◆ Commander Wesley A. Brown was the first African American who graduated from the Naval Academy in 1949.
◆ Vice Admiral Samuel Lee Gravely Jr., was the first African American to take command of a Navy fighting ship in 1962, the USS *Falgout*. In 1971, he also became the first to become an admiral.

Admiral Michelle Howard became the first African-American woman to command a Navy ship, the USS *Rushmore*, in 1999. She became the first African-American woman to achieve four-star rank in the US Armed Forces and

Michelle Howard: First for Women and African Americans

The daughter of an Air Force master sergeant, Admiral Michelle Howard graduated from the Naval Academy in 1982 and served in increasingly more responsible positions as a surface warfare officer. She was the first African-American woman to command a Navy ship, and she was the first African-American woman to achieve three-star rank and four-star rank in the US Armed Forces. She currently serves as the Vice Chief of Naval Operations, the second highest-ranking uniformed person in the US Navy.

became the Vice Chief of Naval Operations, the second highest-ranking uniformed person in the US Navy, in 2014.

By 1992, African Americans represented a larger percentage of the Navy's population than they did of the general US population, clearly a sign that the US Navy is a career path full of opportunity for minorities.

Hispanic Americans, Asian Americans, American Indians, Arab Americans, and many other minority groups have also made major contributions to the US Navy. Hispanics have served in every US conflict since the American Revolution. Civil War Admiral David Farragut, who helped defeat the Confederates at the Battle of Mobile Bay, was of Spanish descent. The Honorable Everett Alvarez Jr., a Mexican American, was the longest-held prisoner of war in North Vietnam. He was a captive for eight-and-a-half years.

While Filipinos have been serving in the US Navy since the 1800s, it was not until Susan Ahn Cuddy, a Korean American, became a female gunnery officer and intelligence officer in World War II that the US Navy could claim its first Asian American in its ranks. Rear Admiral Joseph J. Clark, a Cherokee, was the first American Indian to graduate from the Naval Academy.

Gays in the Navy

The Navy (and the entire Department of Defense) acknowledges that many homosexuals have served honorably and with distinction over the course of the nation's history, but gay men and women were prohibited from openly serving until 2010, when the ban on gays serving in the military was removed. All gay and bisexual men and women can now serve openly in all branches of the military.

SO YOU WANT TO SERVE IN THE NAVY?

"I do solemnly swear that I will support and defend the Constitution of the United States against all enemies, foreign and domestic; that I will bear true faith and allegiance to the same; and that I will obey the orders of the President of the United States and the orders of the officers appointed over me, according to the regulations and the Uniform Code of Military Justice. So help me God."

Oath of Enlistment, recited by every man or woman who commits to naval service.[1]

The Elimination of the Draft

During times of war and from 1948 to 1973, the United States used the "draft" as a way to fill the ranks of the Navy, Army, Air Force, Marines, and Coast Guard. The draft was a requirement that all men register for military service when they turned eighteen years old; if they were called up to serve, they were obligated to do so by law. There were numerous volunteers for service, but the majority of servicemen (and it was just men who were eligible) were "drafted" involuntarily.

But that all changed when the draft was eliminated and America adopted a policy of the "all-volunteer" service. Men are still required to register with the government Service when they turn eighteen years old, but they are not drafted. The work of the US military—including the Navy—is all completed by dedicated volunteers. Most military leaders and the civilians who oversee them agree that the "all-volunteer" force is much better trained for and dedicated to the job.

Are You Eligible?

You must be at least eighteen years old, a United States citizen, and a high-school graduate to join the Navy. If you want to be an officer, you must have a college degree or be working toward one. You also must meet some physical requirements—some are general, some are job-specific. For instance, to be a pilot, you must have good eyesight; to be a Navy SEAL, you must pass some difficult physical fitness tests and you must be an excellent swimmer.

Some jobs in the Navy demand a certain educational background; for instance, to be a submarine officer, a strong educational discipline in engineering and science is required.

All jobs in the Navy require you to be drug free. There is no tolerance for drug use in the Navy, and you will be immediately disqualified if you use drugs. During the course of your naval service, you will be routinely and randomly tested for drugs. Any evidence of drugs will result in an automatic dishonorable discharge. A dishonorable discharge can affect your ability to be hired for civilian jobs and can prevent you from receiving veteran's benefits.

Being in the Navy also requires that you be physically fit; semiannual physical readiness tests (PRTs) are administered to every sailor in the Navy. You must pass this test twice a year in order to remain in the Navy. Maintaining a healthy, balanced diet, exercising regularly, and not smoking will put you on the right path to a successful career in the Navy.

First Step: Find a Recruiter

The first step to joining the Navy is to contact a Navy recruiter, and you can find one on the Navy's recruiting Web site: http://www.navy.com. A recruiter's job is to help interested young men and women become enlisted sailors and officers. The recruiter guides candidates through the application and selection process.

Once you are selected for service—either as an enlisted sailor or as an officer—you must go through intensive training. Enlisted personnel are required to successfully complete Navy "boot camp," a ten-week, full-time training course that teaches new recruits how to wear a uniform and work on a ship. It also offers a detailed indoctrination into the rules and policies governing naval service.

For those people who pursue a career as an officer, there are three ways to receive a commission: the US Naval

Recruiting for the US Navy begins early. In an effort to draw interest from youth, naval personnel visit elementary schools to educate children about a career in the US Navy.

Academy, Naval Reserve Officers' Training Corps (NROTC), and Officers' Candidate School (OCS). The Naval Academy is the most time intensive and demanding of the options, as it requires individuals to commit themselves to naval training full-time for four years, but the Naval Academy also provides a free college education. The NROTC option allows individuals to attend any university to which they are accepted and gives them part-time naval officer training while attending college. Some NROTC candidates also receive free college tuition. OCS gives college graduates the opportunity to become officers by attending thirteen weeks of full-time training.

Next Step: Boot Camp

Once you are selected to join the Navy as an enlisted sailor or as an officer, successful completion of "boot camp" or an officer-training program is required. At boot camp, a recruit is trained on both land and at sea. He or she must pass a series of physical tests that include push-ups, sit-ups, and a one-and-a-half-mile run. There are also swimming tests, which include entering the water from at least five feet above, remaining afloat for five minutes, and swimming at least fifty yards. The recruit will learn first aid, communications, and how to identify different ships and aircraft. About halfway

Recruits march as a division at Recruit Training Command, the Navy's boot camp.

through boot camp, recruits are taught how to fire weapons, including an M6 and a 12-gauge shotgun. On board a ship, firefighting and other damage-control skills are learned and tested.

The final challenge for Navy recruits is the "Battle Stations" test. This exercise has twelve different stages and tests a recruit's knowledge and physical ability gained during boot camp. During the whole Battle Stations test, men and women wear a "Recruit" baseball cap. However, once they complete the challenge, they have the honor of wearing the "Navy" cap. This signifies their transformation into sailors. Following Battle Stations, the recruits graduate in full

Naval personnel must undergo weapons qualification exercises. Here, machine guns are fired aboard the guided-missile destroyer USS *Farragut*.

A recruit division sings as they successfully complete the final leg of a battle stations drill.

uniform at a dignified ceremony, ready to begin their careers in the Navy.

Afterward, each sailor must complete extensive training that will prepare him or her specifically for a designated specialty. This training can last several months or several years, depending on the type of specialty pursued. For example, a Navy pilot can spend several years training almost full-time to learn to fly a fighter aircraft. Even then, a Navy pilot is considered a novice until he or she spends a few years in the fleet, earning experience at sea and in combat. However, pilot is only one of the career choices someone can pursue. There are a variety of other options available to a recently graduated sailor.

Newly commissioned Navy Corps officers toss their hats in the air at the close of the US Naval Academy graduation ceremony.

Job Demands

Serving in the Navy is a dangerous profession. The job requires traveling far from home for long periods of time and fighting enemies of the United States. The Global War on Terrorism has made the work even more dangerous. Many Navy men and women have been killed or wounded in the line of duty. However, those individuals who volunteer for the challenge can find that a career in the Navy can offer skills, education, travel, friendships, and a tremendous amount of responsibility at a very young age.

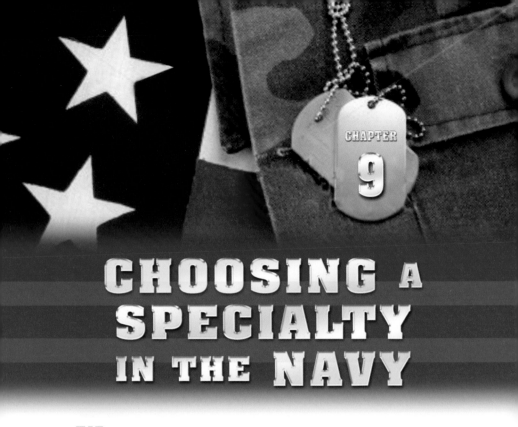

CHOOSING A SPECIALTY IN THE NAVY

While all Navy recruits train for service at sea on a ship, they also undergo extensive training for their chosen specialty—aviation, surface ships, submarines, medical, intelligence, construction engineering, legal, or supply—just to name a few. Each specialty within the Navy offers Sailors a path of increasing responsibilities and demonstrated skills over the course of a twenty-year career.

Flying for the Navy

Since 1910, when Eugene Ely catapulted his plane from the platform of a ship for the first time, the Navy has produced several generations of highly qualified aviators who are proud to wear the Navy "Wings of Gold."

Naval officers who choose aviation can become pilots and fly the aircraft or they can become Naval Flight Officers

(NFOs) and control the aircraft's weapons and guidance systems. This highly trained group of officers can find themselves performing a variety of missions for the Navy—either on ship-based jets or on land-based transport planes. Missions include fleet air defense, air-to-air fighting, ground attack, antisubmarine warfare, and search-and-rescue.

Those who wish to become pilots or NFOs must first become naval officers before they can attend primary flight training and advanced flight training. Because their training is longer and more specialized, these highly respected pilots and NFOs also have longer service obligations.

A naval flight officer lands an aircraft on the flight deck of the aircraft carrier USS *George H.W. Bush*.

WING COMMANDER
M. "WOLFY"

A pilot confirms the weight of his jet prior to launch on the flight deck of the Nimitz-class aircraft carrier USS *John C. Stennis*.

Naval aviation also has a large support crew of technically trained enlisted personnel who specialize in aircraft mechanics, weapons handling, navigation, meteorology, flight safety, and engine systems specialists. Naval aviation cannot operate without them.

Serving on Surface Ships

Command at sea is the goal of many naval officers. Surface warfare officers (SWOs) are those who train their whole careers to command a war-fighting surface ship—to control all operations and supervise the entire crew. After commissioning, those naval officers who want to be SWOs are sent immediately to work aboard a surface ship. While assigned to their first ship, they attend Surface Warfare Officers School (SWOS) and continue to go to sea in increasingly responsible roles in a variety of surface ships—including destroyers, cruisers, frigates, minesweepers, aircraft carriers, patrol boats, supply ships, and oilers. Today's Navy SWOs have a proud legacy in our nation's history.

But surface ships could not operate without its dedicated crew of highly trained enlisted specialists, including boatswain's mates, operations specialists—electrician's mates, enginemen, machinist's mates, fire-control technicians, intelligence specialists, quartermasters, signalmen, and yeomen —just to name a few.

Serving in Submarines

Since Admiral Hyman Rickover launched the USS *Nautilus* in 1955, the US Navy has maintained a fleet of nuclear submarines. It currently has two design types that are on duty under

Quartermaster Third Class Sarah Eleazer plots the position of the USS *Theodore Roosevelt* on a chart table on the navigation bridge, while the aircraft carrier is underway in the Persian Gulf.

the ocean 24 hours a day, 365 days a year: fast-attack submarines (SSNs) and ballistic missile submarines (SSBNs). The SSN-688 Los Angeles class fast-attack submarine is considered the backbone of our Navy's attack submarine force. They travel on the open ocean at high speeds, silently patrolling the seas and quietly observing enemy activity. They are 360 feet long, can travel at 20 plus knots, and can carry 133 people. The US Navy currently has sixty-two of these submarines.

The SSN-21 Seawolf class fast-attack submarine is designed specifically to perform high-speed, submerged, deep-depth operations, and they are much quieter than the Los Angeles class submarines. The US Navy currently has two of these submarines in operation in the fleet today.

The Ohio-class Trident-fleet ballistic-missile submarine (SSBN) is part of America's nuclear force, capable of carrying nuclear weapons and responding to any enemy nuclear threat. They are 560 feet long, can travel submerged at more than 20 knots, and can carry 155 people.

Naval officers who wish to learn how to command a nuclear-powered fast-attack or ballistic-missile submarine must attend nuclear power school and submarine officer basic course. Most submarine officers have strong technical, science, or engineering educational backgrounds.

There is a large support crew of highly trained enlisted personnel who also work on submarines. These specialists include sonar technicians (responsible for listening to and detecting underwater movement of other ships and submarines) weapons handlers, cryptologists (responsible for collecting and analyzing intelligence data) oceanographic specialists, weather forecasters, and nuclear power-plant

Fighting in the "Littorals"

As more conflicts are being fought close to shore (as opposed to out on the open ocean), the United States is investing more resources to build ships that can operate in more shallow waters. The first Littoral Combat Ship (LCS) has been aptly named USS *Freedom*. It is smaller than traditional surface ships, which makes it faster—it can travel at more than forty knots—and easier to maneuver in shallow waters currently inaccessible to conventional naval ships. It has different modules that can be reconfigured to suit several types of missions. The LCS is capable of landing special operations and maritime interdiction forces, as well as intelligence and reconnaissance teams. It also carries helicopters, small boats, and unmanned air, surface, and subsurface vehicles.

The Littoral Combat Ship USS *Freedom* can easily maneuver in shallow waters.

Sonar Technician (Surface) 1st Class Jessica Bonilla stands the surface warfare coordinator watch in the combat information center aboard the Ticonderoga-class guided-missile cruiser USS *Cowpens*.

technicians. Submarines could not operate without the entire crew of individuals.

Navy Medical Professionals

The Navy has a team of medical professionals—doctors, nurses, dentists, hospital corpsmen, and medical service corps—all of whom provide care for the Navy and the Marines. These individuals are highly trained, often by the Navy. In exchange for advanced medical training, they agree to serve in the Navy for several years, caring for fellow servicemen and women.

Submarines and SEALs Working Together

The Navy has recently built several new types of submarines: the Virginia class (SSN-774) of fast-attack submarines, the Seawolf-class (SSN-21) of attack submarines, and a modified Trident ballistic missile submarine—now called a guided missile submarine, or SSGN. The Virginia-class SSN performs many of the same missions as the Los Angeles class submarines, but is specifically designed for littoral (near the shoreline) and regional operations. The Seawolf submarines are exceptionally quiet and fast, is equipped with advanced sensors, and can carry up to fifty weapons in its torpedo room. The SSGNs have been reconfigured to carry up to 154 Tomahawk land-attack missiles, giving the submarine the ability to conduct large-volume strikes—with surprise. These ships are also able to support a Special Operations Force (SOF) of up to sixty-six individuals.

Medical personnel in the Navy have dual roles as combat-trained naval officers and sailors *and* as caregivers to the sick and injured. This dual responsibility makes those who serve in Navy medicine unique professionals.

While most of the Navy's doctors become medical specialists, they are—first and foremost—military physicians, and they all must be prepared to deploy and work in operational or emergency medicine. Pediatrician Lieutenant Commander Julie Kellogg recently returned from a deployment to Iraq with the Second Force Service Support Group. She found herself caring for a large number of Marine Corps casualties from Nasriye, Iraq, at the start of the ground war in Iraq in 2003. As she described it:

> While we did take care of some children, our primary purpose was to care for injured Iraqis and Marine service members. . . . It was very busy for about ten days. The helicopters would bring in injured patients, either a combination of Iraqis and/or Marines, some Iraqi civilians and some Iraqi prisoners-of-war.[1]

The physical conditions of the work made the job even harder.

> We were in one of the biggest sandstorms that they had had in a very long time, so that affected not only our living situation, but also our ability to care for the patients. The helicopters just would not fly, so the incoming patients were held up until the sandstorm let up. Once it did, they all came in at once and it was very intense. . . . What I remember the most about [the injured Marines] was that they wanted to be treated and to go back, if possible. And, of course, many of them couldn't.[2]

Hospital corpsmen serve a unique role in the Navy and in support of the Marine Corps. In combat, they serve as the on-site emergency medical technicians (EMTs) who provide triage and first aid to wounded and sick servicemen and women.

Hospital Corpsman Second Class Jason Deaver has served in the Navy for more than eight years. He specializes as an X-ray technician. He recently returned from a deployment with the Second Medical Battalion out of Camp LeJeune, North Carolina. He was sent to Iraq and was on the

What Do Hospital Corpsmen Do?

The Bluejackets Manual, a sailor's handbook about the Navy, describes a Hospital Corpsman's (HM's) role as follows:

> *HMs assist medical professionals in providing health care to service people and their families. They act as pharmacists, medical technicians, food-service personnel, nurses' aides, physicians' or dentists' assistants, battlefield medics, X-ray technicians, and more. Their work falls into several categories: first aid and minor surgery, patient transportation, patient care, prescriptions and laboratory work, food-service inspections, and clerical duties.*[3]

scene when a suicide bomb exploded in a crowded mess hall in Mosul, Iraq, on December 21, 2004. Twenty-two people were killed and more than sixty people were wounded in the daytime attack during mealtime. Deaver describes his experience with one of the victims of that blast:

> *I had one patient who was in the Army and he had been stationed in Iraq for a year and a half. He was getting ready to go home. He had just gotten off e-mail with his wife. Their anniversary was coming up, he had two kids, and he went to eat chow [lunch] and it exploded. When he came to me, he had a really bad abdomen injury, so he was losing a lot of blood and he actually kept saying to me, "I'm not gonna make it, I'm not gonna make it." I told him he was.*[4]

Deaver said his patient was close to dying and that he lost a lot of blood, but he survived. "I was one of three people that played a role in making sure that he would be around to see his kids grow up."[5]

His patient made a full recovery, but this does not always happen. Today's medical professionals deployed to Iraq and Afghanistan are caring for patients with serious injuries every day. Caring for those in harm's way is hard work—both physically and emotionally.

Navy Nurses

Founded in 1908, the Navy Nurse Corps has a rich history of providing medical care at hospitals, clinics, on board ships, and in field hospitals around the world. These dedicated men and women work closely with Navy medical officers, dental officers, and hospital corpsmen. Like civilian nurses, Navy nurses can find themselves working in emergency room and trauma medicine, general surgery, neurosurgery, obstetrics/gynecology, orthopedics, pediatrics, or psychiatry.

Navy Dentists

Established by Congress in 1912, the Navy Dental Corps is a proud group of dental professionals who are pioneering leading-edge dental techniques and advanced technology, including the high-speed air-turbine hand piece and ultrasonic vibrating instruments. With fourteen Naval Dental Centers around the United States, Puerto Rico, Guam, Italy, and Japan—plus dental officers and dental hygienists on board most large ships, the Navy is capable of providing on-site dental care to its service members assigned all over the world.

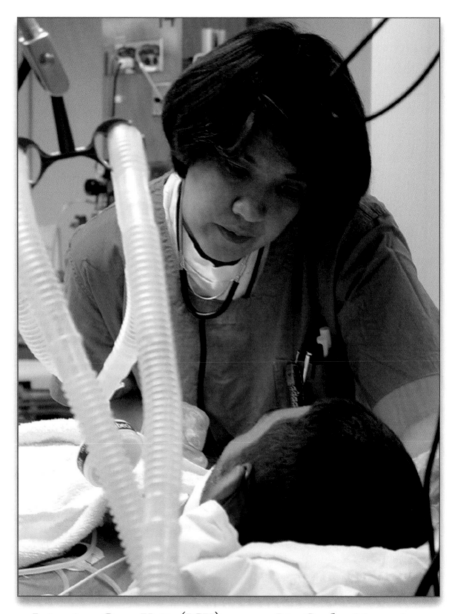

Intensive Care Unit (ICU) nurse Lt. Cmdr. Mary Ann Brantley, Nurse Corps, works on a patient in the ICU aboard the Military Sealift Command hospital ship USNS *Comfort.*

There are several ways to become a Navy medical or dental professional. For aspiring doctors, dentists, and nurses, you can apply for programs to have the Navy pay for your education in return for service in the Navy. You can attend a civilian university for your medical, nursing, or dental degree, or you can apply to attend the Uniformed Services University of the Health Sciences (USUHS), the military's own medical and graduate nursing school in Bethesda, Maryland. Through special programs the Navy offers, you can have your entire medical or dental education funded by the Navy. In return, you agree to serve in the Navy for a specified number of years.

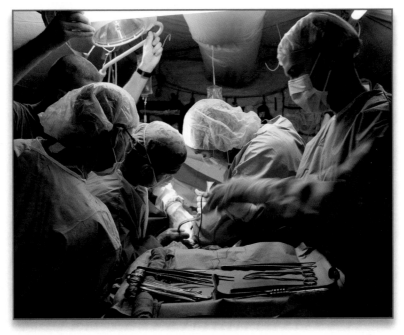

US Navy surgeons and hospital corpsman assigned to the Surgical/Shock Trauma Platoon at Camp Taqaddum in Iraq operate on a Marine injured by an improvised explosive device.

Beyond the Call of Duty: A Sailor Saves Lives under Fire

It was trial by fire—literally. A roadside explosion had just rocked the 1st Marine Division's mobile command-and-control unit on a dusty desert road near Ramadi, Iraq. Hospital Corpsman Second Class Andrew Slaughter was assigned to this Marine division and was responsible for these Marines' medical care. He had no time to think, as immediate medical attention was critical. Sprinting seventy-five yards to the middle of the road where an injured Marine lay, Slaughter performed his first tracheotomy. He stayed focused on opening the Marine's airway while a second explosion rattled the already shell-shocked unit. Again, Slaughter went to work, commandeering an Army Humvee to race across the desert to another burning vehicle—only to find his roommate severely injured. Slaughter patched him up as well.

Two weeks later, his unit was hit again—this time by enemy gunfire. For the third time in less than a month, Slaughter found himself treating casualties—this time in the midst of bullets whizzing by his head. When he finished tending to injuries, he grabbed his 9 mm pistol and killed two Iraqis who were twenty feet away from him.

"I did what I had to do," Slaughter said in an interview. "If I were to freeze . . . they would lose faith in their corpsman." For his heroic actions, Slaughter received the Bronze Star with Combat "V," the highest award given to his platoon.[6]

Some candidates have already earned their degrees before they enter the Navy. All selected for their respective programs are sent to Officer Indoctrination School (OIS), which is a crash course in how to be a naval officer. In five weeks, the Navy trains you in management styles, leadership techniques, Navy history and policies, and how to wear a uniform.

Navy Construction Battalions

Naval Mobile Construction Battalions (NMCBs), or SeaBees, provide critical engineering support for the Navy. These highly trained construction specialists can be deployed anywhere around the world to build airfields, staging areas, hospitals, bridges, and many other logistical structures in support of the Navy and the Marine Corps.

SEALs and Special Operations

Arguably the most disciplined specialties in the Navy, and one of the most dangerous of Navy professions, Navy SEALs must be prepared to operate in any arena—SEa, Air or Land. This is where their name originates. SEALs endure some of the toughest training in the world.

The training required to become a SEAL is extremely demanding, both mentally and physically, and produces the world's best maritime warriors. Those interested in becoming a SEAL must first go to boot camp and learn to be a sailor (or become an officer). Then, SEAL candidates undergo a six-month training program called Basic Underwater Demolition/SEAL (BUD/S) Training in Coronado, California. This six-month course of instruction focuses on physical conditioning, small boat handling, diving physics,

US Navy SEALs conduct delivery vehicle training.

basic diving techniques, land warfare, weapons, demolitions, communications, and reconnaissance.

Navy Lawyers

Yes, there was a television show based on the work of judge advocate generals—or JAGs. These are the military's dedicated team of lawyers. As a Navy JAG corps officer, you can be in a courtroom within one hundred twenty days of beginning active duty. All major commands have JAGs, who are trained as both military officers and as lawyers to advise personnel on all legal matters. They perform legal assistance duties in consumer protection, real estate transactions, federal and state taxes, domestic disputes, and financial counseling. Military and maritime law is different from civilian law and requires specially trained individuals.

Navy Supply Corps Professionals

This highly trained group of professionals performs executive-level duties in financial management, inventory control, physical distribution systems, contracting, computer systems, material logistics, retailing, and food service. They are the officers who order the petroleum, the hamburgers, the ammunition, *and* the toilet paper on board aircraft carriers and other ships. Without supply-corps officers' expertise in inventory, logistics, and distribution systems, the US Navy's ships, bases, and other facilities could not function.

Navy Intelligence Professionals

The Navy's intelligence officers are the individuals who track, collect, and analyze knowledge about an enemy's capabilities and plans. They are commissioned officers who hold a college degree, and they receive very specialized training. They can find themselves working in embassies around the world, on board ships, and in the Pentagon. Intelligence specialists are the enlisted personnel who also work in this field in support of the intelligence officers, preparing charts and reports.

Navy Chaplains and Other Specialists

These are the Navy's religious leaders, representing many faiths. For two hundred twenty-eight years, the Navy's Chaplain Corps has been assigned to hospitals, ships, the Marine Corps, and the Coast Guard and is responsible for providing religious support and counseling services to servicemen and women during war and peacetime. Religious program specialists are the enlisted personnel who support Navy chaplains with administrative and budgetary tasks.

Sailors assigned to the guided missile destroyer USS *Laboon* track and gather intelligence on a known enemy submarine.

The also Navy employs a variety of other specialists—most of whom receive their training in the Navy. This includes divers, photographers, journalists, security guards, cooks and chefs, small-boat handlers, musicians, postal clerks, sonar and radar technicians, electricians, meteorologists, firefighters, navigators, information technology (IT) specialists, construction workers, accountants, and teachers. The Navy usually trains those who enlist right after high school for these jobs. All perform vital roles for the Navy at sea and ashore.

Navy Reserves

The Naval Act of 1920 formally created the Naval and Marine Corps Reserves, a vital component of the Navy that increases its forces in time of war or national emergency. The reserves provide a backup component to active duty forces. These part-time sailors serve one weekend a month and two full weeks a year to fulfill their service obligation and to maintain their Navy skills while working their civilian jobs.

As of September 11, 2001, the role of the Navy Reserves (and the other services' reserve forces) has significantly changed. More reservists are being "called up" and sent overseas for months at a time to help the Navy when it has a shortage of personnel.

The Navy-Marine Corps Relationship

While the Marine Corps and the Navy are separate, uniformed services, the Marine Corps does fall under the Department of the Navy, and its mission is to provide the Navy with landing forces for amphibious and land-based operations.[7] The Marine Corps and the Navy have a

Sailors conduct training aboard a 34-foot Sea Ark Navy security boat on the York River.

historically close relationship. The Navy relies on the Marine Corps to project sea power ashore, and the Marine Corps depends on the Navy to transport them to and support them in expeditionary missions around the world. Navy hospital corpsman also provide medical care for Marine Corps units.

The Navy-Coast Guard Relationship

The smallest of the military services, the Coast Guard is a military, maritime service within the Department of Homeland Security (DHS) in peacetime. In wartime, or by direction of the president, the Coast Guard serves under the Department of the Navy. Members of the Coast Guard

The US Coast Guard serves under the naval department in times of war. It is the duty of the Coast Guard to patrol our waters and to keep them safe.

protect US harbors, inland waterways, and coasts. They perform search-and-rescue missions, ensure maritime safety, and provide navigational landmarks throughout the nation's forty thousand miles of waterways.[8] Since September 11, 2001, the Coast Guard has taken on a more global role. At the height of Operation Iraqi Freedom, there were more than twelve hundred fifty Coast Guard personnel deployed to the Persian Gulf and central Europe in support of the war on terrorism.

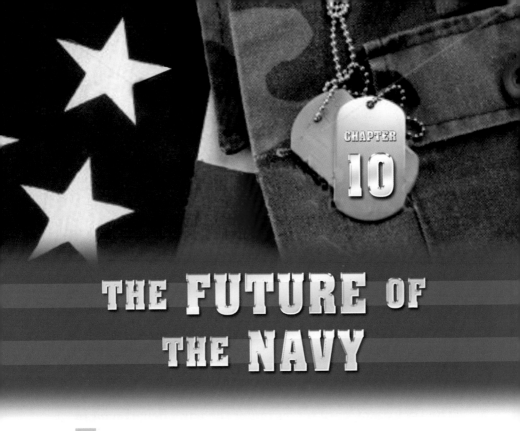

THE **FUTURE** OF THE **NAVY**

CHAPTER

10

The Global War on Terrorism has tested and taxed all the military services—requiring its personnel to deploy many times over the last fourteen years. These overseas assignments have resulted in long and arduous duty at sea and in combat in Iraq, Afghanistan, Yemen, the Philippines, and many other countries. Navy Sailors who have volunteered for these assignments have endured long trips away from their families and friends and the comforts of home in the United States.

The Navy will still have ships and aircraft and submarines patrolling the oceans, but they have also begun using ships and riverine vessels that can patrol the coastal and inland waterways in foreign countries. The Navy is also deploying unmanned vehicles—or "drones," which are remote-controlled devices that can observe enemy activity on land, at sea, and under the water—without putting a single sailor at risk. In the future, it might not be uncommon to see Navy aircraft carriers with Air Force planes and Army helicopters, as the entire military seeks to work more closely together in the future. Undoubtedly, the Navy will increasingly use its special operations forces—those people who are specially trained in urban warfare, hostage rescue, and highly secret operations in very small groups.

Of course, the future is always uncertain, but planning for and building ships, submarines, aircraft, and weapons that are flexible and agile are keys to the future ability of the United States Navy to respond to, and hopefully prevent,

The US Air Force, Navy and Marine Corps work together to locate, track, and engage units at sea, in the air, on land, and in cyberspace.

future conflicts. Likewise, the nation's ability to prepare its *people* for the future is also critical to success Those individuals who want to join the Navy of the future must prepare to be physically fit, eager to learn new skills, and be flexible to tackle a variety of jobs.

Just over the ocean's horizon, the US Navy is underway, defending our military forces overseas, ensuring that merchant ships can safely transport goods around the world, and fighting terrorists. What will the US Navy look like years from now?

The Sailor's Creed

I am a United States Sailor.

I will support and defend the Constitution of the United States of America and I will obey the orders of those appointed over me.

I represent the fighting spirit of the Navy and those who have gone before me to defend freedom and democracy around the world.

I proudly serve my country's Navy combat team with Honor, Courage, and Commitment.

I am committed to excellence and the fair treatment of all.[1]

APPENDIX:
US NAVY PAY SCALE

Officer and Enlisted Pay Grades, Ranks, Pay Scales,* and Insignia

Enlisted			
Pay Grade	Rank	Pay Scale	Insignia
E-1	Seaman Recruit	$1,547	
E-2	Seaman Apprentice	$1,734	
E-3	Seaman	$1,823–$2,055	
E-4	Petty Officer Third Class	$2,019–$2,451	
E-5	Petty Officer Second Class	$2,202–$3,125	
E-6	Petty Officer First Class	$2,404–$3,724	
E-7	Chief Petty Officer	$2,780–$4,996	
E-8	Senior Chief Petty Officer	$3,999–$5,703	
E-9	Master Chief Petty Officer	$4,885–$7,585	

Naval Officers			
Pay Grade	Rank	Pay Scale	Insignia
O-1	Ensign	$2,934–$3,692	
O-2	Lieutenant Junior Grade	$3,380–$4,678	
O-3	Lieutenant	$3,912–$6,365	
O-4	Lieutenant Commander	$4,449–$7,430	
O-5	Commander	$5,157–$8,762	
O-6	Captain	$6,186–$10,952	
O-7	Rear Admiral (lower half)	$8,264–$12,347	
O-8	Rear Admiral (upper half)	$9,946–$14,338	
O-9	Vice Admiral	$14,056–17,436	
O-10	Admiral	$16,072–$19,762	

* Pay is shown as monthly without any benefits/bonuses.

Warrant Officer Pay Grades, Ranks, Pay Scales,* and Insignia

Enlisted			
Pay Grade	Rank	Pay Scale	Insignia
W-1	Warrant Officer	$2,868–$4,956	
W-2	Chief Warrant Officer	$3,267–$5,453	
W-3	Chief Warrant Officer	$3,692–$6,477	
W-4	Chief Warrant Officer	$4,043–$7,531	
W-5	Chief Warrant Officer	$7,189–$9,408	

US Navy pilots show the "Fly Navy" slogan in the International Space Station.

TIMELINE

OCTOBER 13, 1775—US Navy is founded.

SEPTEMBER 23, 1779—Commodore John Paul Jones and his ship, the *Bonhomme Richard*, defeat the HMS *Serapis* off the coast of England during the Revolutionary War.

FEBRUARY 16, 1804—Lieutenant Stephen Decatur slips into Tripoli Harbor and destroys the *Philadelphia* without a single loss.

AUGUST 19, 1812—The *Constitution* earns its nickname Old Ironsides when she defeats the frigate HMS *Guerrière* during the War of 1812.

SEPTEMBER 10, 1813—Master Commandant Oliver Hazard Perry defeats the British in the Battle of Lake Erie.

MARCH 29, 1844—Uriah Levy, the Navy's first Jewish officer, is promoted to captain. He is credited with eliminating flogging (beating) in the Navy.

OCTOBER 10, 1845—The US Naval Academy is established.

MARCH 9, 1862—The *Monitor* and the *Virginia* (formerly the *Merrimack*) duel in the first battle of ironclads during the Civil War.

AUGUST 5, 1864—Rear Admiral David Farragut successfully defeats Confederate forces in the Battle of Mobile Bay.

SEPTEMBER 11, 1872—James Henry Conyers becomes the first African American to attend the US Naval Academy.

FEBRUARY 15, 1898—The battleship *Maine* is destroyed in Havana Harbor, sparking the Spanish-American War.

Timeline

MAY 1, 1898—Commodore George Dewey defeats the Spanish in the Battle of Manila Bay.

NOVEMBER 14, 1910—Eugene Ely flies the first aircraft launched from a ship.

MARCH 20, 1922—The Navy builds the USS *Langley* (CV 1), the first aircraft carrier.

DECEMBER 7, 1941—The Japanese attack Pearl Harbor.

JUNE 4–6, 1942—The US Navy sinks four Japanese carriers in the Battle of Midway during World War II.

JUNE 6, 1944—The United States and the Allies invade Normandy, in the largest amphibious assault ever—with more than twenty-five hundred US Navy ships and crafts involved.

SEPTEMBER 15, 1950—Marines land at Inchon in a surprise attack against the North Koreans during the Korean War.

JANUARY 17, 1955—The world's first nuclear-powered submarine, the USS *Nautilus*, gets underway for the first time.

MAY 5, 1961—Commander Alan B. Shepard becomes the first American in space.

OCTOBER 1962—President John Kennedy orders a naval blockade to prevent the Soviets from sending in nuclear missiles, resulting in the Cuban Missile Crisis.

AUGUST 1964—President Lyndon Johnson orders the US Navy to bomb North Vietnam in response to supposed attacks on US Navy ships in the Gulf of Tonkin, escalating the Vietnam War.

AUGUST 17, 1990—US naval forces are sent to the Persian Gulf to enforce UN sanctions against Iraq—in response to Iraq's invasion of Kuwait.

JANUARY 19, 1991—The submarine USS *Louisville* (SSN 724) launches the first submerged Tomahawk guided missile.

OCTOBER 1994—Women are allowed to deploy on the USS *Dwight D. Eisenhower* (CVN-69) as part of the crew for the first time.

SEPTEMBER 11, 2001—The World Trade Center towers in New York City and the Pentagon are attacked by terrorists.

OCTOBER 7, 2001—US forces attack Afghanistan. Naval forces participate, including surface ships launching Tomahawk missiles, aircraft carriers launching air strikes, and Navy SEALs performing special operations missions.

2010—The Secretary of Defense repeals the ban on homosexuals in the military, allowing gays to openly serve in all services.

MAY 2, 2011—A small group of Navy SEALs assassinate Osama bin Laden, the terrorist who orchestrated the September 11, 2001, attacks on the World Trade Center twin towers and the Pentagon.

2013—The Secretary of Defense repeals the restrictions on women in combat, opening up thousands of positions in the military.

CHAPTER NOTES

CHAPTER 1   The Lone Survivor

1. "Famous Navy Quotes: Who Said Them . . . and When," *Naval Historical Center*, July 20, 2005, <http://www.history.navy.mil/trivia.trivia/2.htm> (September 13, 2006).
2. Luttrell, Marcus. *Lone Survivor: The Eyewitness Account of Operation RedWing and The Lost Heroes of SEAL Team 10* (New York: Little, Brown and Company), p. 231.

CHAPTER 2   Fighting the British for Independence

1. "Founding Fathers: John Paul Jones," *Liberty Matters Journal*, July 1998, <http://www.libertymatters.org/libertymattersjournal/31.htm> (September 13, 2006).
2. Ibid.
3. E.B. Potter, *Sea Power: A Naval History*, 2nd ed. (Annapolis, Md.: Naval Institute Press, 1981), p. 85.
4. "Stephen Decatur," *Naval Historical Center*, June 8, 2001, <http://www.history.navy.mil/faqs/faq110-1.htm> (September 13, 2006).
5. Nathan Miller, *The US Navy—A History*, 3rd ed. (Annapolis, Md.: US Naval Institute Press, 1997), p. 57.
6. Ellen Fried, "Old Ironsides: Warrior and Survivor," *Prologue Magazine*, Spring 2005, <http://www.archives.gov/publications/prologue/2005/spring/ironsides.html> (September 13, 2006).
7. Craig L. Symonds, *The Naval Institute Historical Atlas of the US Navy* (Annapolis, Md.: US Naval Institute Press, 1995), p. 48.

CHAPTER 3   A Young Nation's Navy Emerges

1. Chester G. Hearn, *The Illustrated Directory of the United States Navy* (St. Paul, Minn.: MBI Publishing, 2003), p. 86.
2. Nathan Miller, *The US Navy—A History*, 3rd ed. (Annapolis, Md.: US Naval Institute Press, 1997), p. 148.
3. E.B. Potter, *Sea Power: A Naval History*, 2nd ed. (Annapolis, Md.: Naval Institute Press, 1981), p. 155.
4. Ibid., pp. 161–162.
5. Theodore Roosevelt, "Naval War College Address, June 2, 1897," *Almanac of Theodore Roosevelt*, July 2, 2006, <http://www.theodore-roosevelt.com/tr1898.htm> (September 13, 2006).
6. Hearn, p. 140.

CHAPTER 4 US Navy Defends Freedom All Over the World

1. Chester G. Hearn, *The Illustrated Directory of the United States Navy* (St. Paul, Minn.: MBI Publishing, 2003), p. 146.
2. E.B. Potter, *Sea Power: A Naval History*, 2nd ed. (Annapolis, Md.: Naval Institute Press, 1981), p. 227.
3. Craig L. Symonds, *The Naval Institute Historical Atlas of the US Navy* (Annapolis, Md.: US Naval Institute Press, 1995), p. 128.
4. Potter, p. 198.
5. Daniel Moran, "Trouble," *Center for Contemporary Conflict*, December 2002, <http://ccc.nps.navy.mil/rsepResources/si/dec02/terrorism.asp> (September 13, 2006).
6. Thomas J. Cutler, *A Sailor's History of the US Navy* (Annapolis, Md.: US Naval Institute Press, 2005), p. 103.
7. James A. Field, Jr., "Foreword," *History of United State Naval Operations: Korea*, May 5, 2000, <http://www.history.navy.mil/books/field/foreword.htm> (September 13, 2006).
8. Hearn, p. 291.
9. Cutler, p. 29.
10. Jamie Howren and Taylor Baldwin Kiland, *Open Doors: Vietnam POWs Thirty Years Later* (Washington, D.C.: Potomac Books, Inc., 2005), pp. 34–35.
11. Cutler, p. 29.
12. Cutler, p. 30.
13. Symonds, p. 212.
14. Sherry Sontag and Christopher Drew, with Annette Lawrence Drew, *Blind Man's Bluff: The Untold Story of American Submarine Espionage* (New York: HarperCollins, 1998), p. xiv.
15. "USS *Louisville* (SSN 724)," *Commander Submarine Force: US Pacific Fleet*, n.d., <http://www.csp.navy. mil/css3/724.htm> (February 3, 2006).
16. Symonds, p. 226.
17. Chief of Naval Operations, "US Navy in Desert Shield/Desert Storm," *Naval Historical Center*, April 24, 2001, <http://www.history.navy.mil/wars/ dstorm/ds5. htm> (June 10, 2005).

CHAPTER 5 Naval Operations Today

1. US Navy, "Vision—Presence—Power: A Program Guide to the US Navy," 2005 ed., p. 54.
2. JO1 Joaquin Juatai, "*Abraham Lincoln* Answers the Call in Banda Aceh," January 30, 2005, < http://www. news.navy.mil/search/display.asp?story_id=16644> (June 10, 2005).
3. Captain Richard Callas, Commanding Officer, USS *Iwo Jima* (LHD-7), in an e-mail on September 12, 2005.

Chapter Notes

4. Mark D. Faram and Andrew Scutro, "Back in Brown: Navy Assembling Riverine Unit to Deploy to Iraq Next Year," *Navy Times,* January 23, 2006, p. 8.
5. Gidget Fuentes, "SEALs' Immediate Future Is on the Ground," *Navy Times,* January 23, 2006, p. 17.

CHAPTER 6   How Is the Navy Organized?

1. *Sea Power: 2005 Almanac,* vol. 48, no. 1, pp. 4–5, January 2005, <http://www.navyleague.org/sea_power/ almanac_jan_05_01.php> (February 20, 2006).
2. http://www.navy.mil/navydata/nav_legacy.asp?id=146.

CHAPTER 7   Diversity in the Navy

1. Susan H. Godson, *Serving Proudly: A History of Women in the US Navy* (Annapolis, Md.: US Naval Institute Press, 2001), p. 1.
2. Ibid., pp. 106, 111.

CHAPTER 8   So You Want to Serve in the Navy?

1. "Before the Navy," *Navy.com,* n.d., <http://www.navy.com/about/before/meps> (September 13, 2006).

CHAPTER 9   Choosing a Specialty in the Navy

1. Phone interview with Lieutenant Commander Julie Kellogg, MC, USN, on April 12, 2005.
2. Ibid.
3. Thomas J. Cutler, *The Bluejackets Manual.* Centennial ed. (Annapolis, Md.: US Naval Institute, 2002), p. 40.
4. Phone interview with HM2 Jason Deaver, USN, on April 12, 2005.
5. Ibid.
6. Gidget Fuentes, "First Aid under Fire," *Navy Times,* April 4, 2005, p. 14.
7. Cutler, p. 551.
8. "US Coast Guard Organization and Missions," *Sea Power: 2005 Almanac,* vol. 48, no. 1, p. 113, January 2005, <http://www.navyleague.org/sea_power/ almanac_jan_05_113.php> (February 20, 2006).

CHAPTER 10   The Future of the Navy

1. "Sailor's Creed," *US Navy Office of Information,* n.d., <http://www.chinfo.navy.mil/navpalib/traditions/html/ sailorscreed.html> (March 6, 2006).

GLOSSARY

Allies (Allied Powers)—The countries that united to fight against Germany in the two world wars.

battery—A group of big military guns.

bridge—Area in the superstructure from which a ship is operated.

Central Powers—The countries, mostly Germany and Austria-Hungary, that joined forces to fight against the Allies in World War I.

collier—A bulk cargo ship that carried coal.

convoy—A group of ships that travel together for safety.

deck—Horizontal planking or plating that divides a ship into layers (never called a floor).

deterrent—A retaliatory means of preventing enemy attack.

envoy—A person who represents his or her government in another country to discuss trade, war, economics, and other international issues; a diplomat.

escort—To accompany for protection.

hatch—An opening in a deck used for access.

insurgent—A person who takes part in a rebellion against an established authority.

knot—Nautical mile per hour.

littoral—Of, relating to, or situated on the shore of the sea or a lake.

magazine—The area on a warship where ammunition is stored.

mizzenmast—The third mast from the bow in a vessel.

moor—To make fast to a pier, another ship, or a mooring buoy; also, to anchor.

Glossary

pitch—Vertical rise and fall of a ship's bow and stern caused by the movement of the sea (when a ship tips forward and backward).

reconnaissance—An inspection of an area to gain information.

stern—The aftermost part of a vessel.

tactical—Strategic.

U-boat—A submarine, although the term usually refers to a German submarine during World Wars I and II.

unmanned aerial vehicle (UAV)—Commonly called a "drone," is an aircraft without a human pilot aboard.

FURTHER READING

Books

Borneman, Walter R. *The Admirals*. New York: Little, Brown and Company, 2012.

Kyle, Chris. *American Sniper*. New York: HarperCollins, 2012.

Owen, Mark. *No Easy Day: The Autobiography of a Navy SEAL*. New York: Penguin Group, 2012.

Rockwood, Malcolm. *United States Navy Boot Camp—The Complete Survival Guide for The Worst Eight Weeks of Your Life!*. Seattle: Amazon Digital Services, Inc., 2014.

Web Sites

history.navy.mil
The Naval History and Heritage Command provides information on museums and collections.

navy.mil
Explore the US Navy's official Web site.

navy.com
Learn more about what it takes to join the US Navy.

Movies

The Hunt for Red October. Directed by John McTiernan. Hollywood, Calif.: Paramount Pictures, 1990.
Thriller about the Navy during the Cold War.

U–571. Directed by Jonathan Mostow. Universal City, Calif.: Universal Pictures, 2000.
A US Navy crew boards a disabled German U-boat to steal the Enigma code.

INDEX